PERSONALITY DISORDER

The Fight of the Fears

PERSONALITY DISORDER

The Fight of the Fears

Megan Florence

Personality Disorder published by Rangitawa Publishing, Feilding, New Zealand 2016

www.rangitawapublishing.com
rgitawa@xtra.co.nz

ISBN 978-0-9941268-8-7

This novel won the 2016 Rangitawa Publishing Young Adult Novel section. Megan Florence completed a Bachclor of Arts in English Literature at Victoria University, Wellington, New Zealand.

Rangitawa
PUBLISHING

Chapter One

Home of the Spirit Ghosts

My name is Saffron. I know, don't laugh, it is a stupid name but my parents thought it was sweet and pretty. I am like any other teenage girl, two legs, two arms, a body, and a spirit ghost. Our histories tell us that humans didn't used to have a ghost. Throughout the ages we have had names for our spirit; minions or familiars, ghosts or shadows, but I'm not a witch and I'm not an alien. We call them personalities for they are what define us. They are not physically attached to us but there is a certain pull that means we cannot function without each other. Our personality looks like an immortal version of ourselves and does not have physical weakness. We share the same thoughts, although no one else can hear what they say, and they are our constant companion. There are four categories that our personalities fall into. History states that these categories are chosen by our innermost workings. They are the categories of the elements; Earth, Fire, Water, and Air. Our personalities look like us as if we were made out of our element. As our moods change our personality's density reflects that change; in fear they pale, in defiance they grow bolder. I guess they would seem magical to anyone else for they do not tire or age with us and they are not tied to gravitational pulls nor weighed down with human flaws of sustenance.

I go to high school like any normal kid my age. I say kid but I am in my last year and will soon have to think about joining the real world. At my graduation it is customary for the graduating girl to choose her husband. I don't want to get married. When I said I am like any other teenage girl, I lied a little. I don't like our customs. You see, our society is split between the traditionalists and the rebels of the new age.

The rebellion happened years ago and resulted in much bloodshed. We learnt about it in history class; the change in government, the hope of a new way of life. The rebellion now is nothing compared to that. Now the rebels are barely heard of and we use it as a label to fight against the oppression of any kind of authority. My parents are traditionalists and believe in the old customs, including the one that states I must marry straight after graduation. For a woman is nothing without a husband. This view in particular is one which leads me to be a rebel of the new age; I refuse to be defined by a male name for I have my own. I am my own person.

My best friend is Blake. We have known each other since we were young. He is in the same year as I am at school. Dark haired with broody eyes, Blake is handsome and will have a big choice to make for when we graduate, he must propose to a girl. The girls must then make their choice on which boy to accept, if anyone proposes to them at all of course. One of the reasons we are so close is that we feel the same way about the customs. He doesn't want to marry either. We spend a lot of time together in the fields talking about these customs as our personalities fight, dance, and fly.

"It's stupid!" he exclaimed one day when we were alone in the meadow.

"I don't want to get married so young, I'm not sure I want to get married at all!"

"And definitely not because someone is forcing us to!" I replied with vehemence.

"Did you see what it said on the news yesterday?" Blake asked.

"No," I replied. I had missed it as dinner had run later than normal due to my parents entertaining some dinner guests.

"It said the rebels have been getting stronger, that they have begun 'forceful recruitment'."

"Forceful recruitment? What does that even mean?"

I turned to face Blake and glimpsed my water personality Beatrice in my peripheral vision dancing through the air with Blake's earth personality Casper.

"People are going missing all over the country. The government are doing all they can, but it isn't enough. They can't stop the rebels from taking people."

I paled. This was not the kind of rebellion I wanted to be a part of. I just wanted my freedom but these rebels were taking that from others. I looked around me. The meadow stretched out in front of us all the way along to the woods. Behind us was the path to the town. No matter which direction I looked, there was not a fence in sight. Physically it seemed I already had my freedom, but it wasn't enough.

Catching my new mood Beatrice had quietened down, watching me intently. The meadow was full of sunlight. Surrounded by fresh grass and wild flowers I couldn't imagine a better place to have my freedom. I looked further into the distance, across to the woods. They cast a shadow that even in the sunlight, looked foreboding. It was always an irrational fear but I never felt comfortable around the woods. Behind where we were sitting the town spread out. Distant traffic sounds reminded us that we weren't far away from control.

"We should just leave Saffy!"

Blake broke through my reverie.

"Just go right through the woods right now and then we would never have to get married."

I started. This wasn't part of our argument. We were supposed to complain about the customs, our parents, The Authority and then, once we had fizzled out, decide that it might not be so bad if we could just figure out a way to appease our parents. It had crossed my mind that it wouldn't be so bad if I married Blake but the idea of standing up and declaring that to everyone had me blushing so bad I couldn't bear the thought. Besides, I didn't know if he would even think to propose to me. He was my best friend but Blake was a lot more popular than I was and there were so many girls prettier than me that would want to marry him. I doubted anyone would propose to me and that thought was even more embarrassing.

The girls who were not proposed to didn't have much of a future. They were usually set to work in a factory and mostly shunned from society. I thought about what he had said. I truly did hate it here. I hate The Authority and its stupid customs. May be I could leave, especially if I could take Blake with me, our own adventure at last.

"Let's do it," I agreed. "But not until we finish school, let's wait until the end of the year."

"It'll be hard to say goodbye to everyone," said Blake, softly.

"Are you backing out already?" I asked.

I was challenging him and I knew he'd accept. I knew the minute I agreed to this adventure that there would definitely be one.

That night I had a dream. This wasn't unusual: I dream a lot and often remember what happened. They were more vivid than normal people's dreams; sometimes I could even tell that I was in a dream. It gets a little confusing when I split my consciousness away from my dream self but it makes for cool stories to tell Blake. He can't control his dreams, which means he's not as good as me. In a competitive friendship this information is everything. My dream that night was scary.

Saffy is amidst hundreds of other people standing in rows, all in uniform.

They are all looking forward with blank expressions and appear to be awaiting a command. It comes from a disembodied voice.

Destroy.

The army moves forward, walking over everything in sight. They seem like giants as one footstep crushes an entire building.

I notice with dull realisation that it is my own town they are crushing. I notice as I crush my own home, then my school. Slowly I watch my town crush to the ground under the feet of my army.

Saffy enjoys this.

Saffy feels a laugh bubbling inside her and so lets it out as she puts a foot down on the church. Soon the entire army is echoing her laughs. Throughout the desolation one building stays intact. Saffy realises it is Blake's house. She turns towards it and finds herself shrinking with every step.

By the time she is outside the door she is small enough to get in. So she does.

Inside is a banqueting hall much too big to fit inside Blake's house. Sitting at the table are all the people of the town. They turn to me as I walk in and ask for my leadership. They seem to want to follow me.

This scares Saffy and she turns to run out the door.

But the door had gone. Replacing that was an open field. I turn back to the leadership-seeking crowd to discover it had turned into an angry mob. Old fashioned, they chased me with pitch forks and torches. They chased me across the meadow but in the dream like style, something was wrong with my legs.

Saffy couldn't run and so had to leap instead. There were great pauses between leaps where the angry mob almost caught up with her before she leaped away in great footsteps.

As she leapt through the meadow, Saffy flashed past wolves, giants, witches, goblins, faeries, and children; each one cackling loudly at her.

The next day I awoke to my alarm going off. I hit snooze and lay in bed thinking over my dream. It wasn't one I would tell Blake about. I got up and went for a shower. While shampooing my hair I thought about my schedule for today. It was Thursday. Thursday's were the worst day of the week: double chemistry followed by calculus, history, geography, and English. The only good but about the day was history. Even lunches weren't fun at the moment as Blake had sports practice at lunchtimes.

Out of the shower I brushed my teeth, dried my hair, and put on my school uniform. Looking at myself in the mirror I put the tiniest hint of lip gloss on. I didn't like wearing make-up and I certainly wasn't interested in that being all that ever mattered to me but deep down I was worried that I would end up as a factory worker so I tried to put a little effort into my appearance, hoping someone would notice me.

Glancing at the clock I realized that as usual, I would have to rush to get to school on time. I raced down the stairs to the kitchen. Mum was getting dad's breakfast while he sat at the kitchen table, drinking a cup of coffee and reading the paper. Something he was reading was making him frown through his reading glasses and shake his head. I kissed Dad on the head and Mum on the cheek and headed back through the door.

"Late for school," I called over my shoulder. I heard Dad laugh as I shut the front door. It was a wonderful sound and made me happy, especially knowing that my mother would have been unimpressed with my appearance and my quick departure from their presence.

I met up with Blake at the corner of the road between his house and school. We met here every morning and walked to school together even though we only had one class together and we never sat with each other. Blake had many friends, all into sports like him. He sat with them in classes and was never around at lunch. He always made time for me before and after school though and I didn't mind being on my own during classes, it was easier to concentrate that way.

"You're late," he said to me, grinning. I couldn't help but notice that next to my flustered and sleepy state, Blake looked cooler and sleeker than ever. We hurried off to school. While I had double chemistry first, Blake had physical education and health so he headed off to the gym and I walked to the science block.

The day seemed to go by incredibly slowly. In history we were learning about a world war from hundreds of years ago. I struggled to see the relevance to our curriculum to learn these stories now but still they were my favourite part of history. Today part of our lecture involved a slide show of pictures. We were concentrating on comparing lives of the soldiers to the lives of the people left behind. There were pictures of starving, dirty people. I noticed how much mud and smoke there was in the pictures despite the age of the photos. Then there were pictures of the trenches. Barbaric conditions of trenches were then contrasted by a massive pile of shoes. This pile of shoes was replaced by a picture of a pile of bodies and soldiers throwing them into a mass grave.

"World War Two was not the last war fought by the entire world but it was the worst," my history teacher was saying. "As you can see on these pictures, conditions were bad for everyone globally with starvation, disease, and death flooding the world. This and the other two world wars were fought because a few men decided their cause justified millions of deaths. There was no winner, no victorious party to these wars as they were fought with innocent blood.

"Now, thanks to The Authority, we are safe in the knowledge that there will be no more war like these and, due to the world wide independence of each country, casualties will always be minimal in any fight. The Authority's continued protection and government allows us to work independently from other countries. Any wars that other countries partake in are of no concern to us and since the revolution that put The Authority into power there have been no civil wars. The people feel no need to fight the government because we have everything we need, unlike the people in these pictures whom suffered a terrible amount of pain."

The class was silent looking at these photos. A text book was handed out and we began to read. Insignificant dates flew off the page at me and the words moved around on the page. I couldn't concentrate because I knew that this information was only needed for my exams and then I could forget about it. History was my favourite class but I knew that it was a pointless class for me to take. I knew that at best I could get a job as a receptionist at a high class office. As the daughter of a higher classed family, there was no need for me to work, especially once I was married. There would never be any real need for my education but I was still expected to get very good grades.

I found history interesting as I loved seeing all the paintings and pictures taken over time. I loved seeing snippets of other people's lives and wondering what it would have been like to live among them. I loved daydreaming about how different my life would have been. The wars were not my favourite subject as it made me nervous to think about so many deaths but, like my teacher had said- "we are safe."

When lunch time finally came around I went straight to the art department. Knowing that Blake was training I wasn't interested in hanging around with any of my class mates. I walked into the studio and sat at one of the benches. I got out my pencil and sketch pad and began to draw. Often when I dream a certain scene would get stuck in my head and wouldn't go away until I had drawn it. I drew last night's dream out- an army of people crushing the town below. It was powerful and dark, influenced by the pictures I had seen in history. I was so engrossed in my art that I almost missed the bell to next class.

Hurriedly, I walked off to English.

Another school day was done and ticked off. Graduation was getting closer and with every day, my future was getting murkier. The chance of becoming a factory worker was getting higher with every lunch I spent in the art studio and with every morning I didn't put on make-up. I knew my mother worried. The shame brought upon the family if I wasn't proposed to would surely break her. It was worrying but it wasn't long before we had more important things to worry about.

Chapter Two

The Authority and its Rules

Over the next few days odd things started happening: more disappearances were reported on the news as the rebels became bolder and bolder with their people snatching. Then the local papers had their own story to report. Our head master at the school disappeared with no explanation of where he was going or why. The papers claimed the rebels had reached our town.

On my way home from school I picked up a paper and read through the article. In the government paper they had added steps and precautions that everyone should take for their own safety;

Follow the rules to keep safe

- Anyone out after nine in the evening does so at their own risk
- One should make sure to travel on Authority approved routes
- One should prevent travelling alone at all costs
- One should avoid travelling unless for work or Authority approved outings
- If someone you know is taken, report to The Authority immediately

- Use Authority approved security systems on houses and businesses
- Keep your personalities on alert at all times

To me these precautions just sounded like more ways for The Authority to keep us under control but it was for our own good.

Despite these precautions, students started disappearing too. Each week more people would be missing. After six months, the town was half empty. Shops were boarded up and the sheriff was working overtime to try and work it out. The town was in a panic.

"What do you think is really going on?" I asked Blake one day. We were back in our meadow, trying to ignore the stress of the new goings on in the town. The sheriff had called in back up and armed Authority Guards were patrolling the streets, adding more fear to the town. Although they were there to protect us, they followed the traditional rules and forced others to comply. They were loud and intimidating, eating our food and drinking the pubs dry.

"I don't know, but I don't like it. It is just like the news said, we have to be careful: 'follow the rules to keep safe'," he said, frowning. "The sooner we get out of here the better."

"Are we still going to go then?" I asked doubtfully. How could we leave our families now that something so drastic had happened in our town? Where could we even go that would be safe?

"Of course, you think that what has happened will stop our families from forcing us into marriage?" he said turning to face me and throwing the blade of grass he'd been playing with."Saffy, if we don't get out now, we'll never escape and we'll end up as sad and boring as them!"

He looked panicked with the thought of turning out like his dad. The fear was justified; Blake's dad was not a pleasant man, especially when he drank. Many times I had seen Blake with bruises on his skin after his dad had had a particularly nasty night drinking. Their home was filled with arguments and fights but his mum never let that show in public. I had tried to convince Blake to get away from his dad but he wouldn't leave his mum alone with him. The fighting and the drinking got worse until a year back when Blake's dad drank himself into an early grave, falling into the river on his way home from the pub. Blake's family had always been strict traditionalists and yet when his dad died, Blake's mother turned inwards, creating a loveless and even stricter home for Blake to live in. Something had her scared and trapped living the way she did before her husband died. Blake had no siblings so life at home was difficult for him at best. He had no love for his late father and we never talked about him. I gave in, knowing he was right. We had to get out.

It was when I got home that I really thought about what I was doing. I was in the kitchen helping Mum cook dinner. I was quietly peeling carrots while she stuffed and wrapped the chicken. It was one of Dad's favourite meals. I was at the sink, my back to the room when my mother spoke to me.

"Saffron?"

She never called me anything but my full name, making me feel like I was always in trouble. "Do not make plans for this Saturday. You and I are going to go shopping and to luncheon with a few ladies and their daughters."

I shuddered and groaned inwardly. Not only did it sound awful but plans with my mother always turned into fights. I tried not to show any signs of disgust hoping to reasonably get her to let me off the hook. I had finished peeling the carrots so I turned to face her.

"Do I have to go? Blake and I were…"

"Blake can wait for another day," My mum interrupted. "It is time you spent some time with some ladies. We can go to the salon and take care of your nails and eyebrows Darling."

I flinched.

"I'm not sure why my eyebrows need taking care of. No one cares what they look like." I turned my back on Mum and picked up the knife. Over the chopping of vegetables Mum replied.

"No one notices when they look good but Darling, everyone notices when they look bad. Sweetheart, Mrs Morrings was telling me over tea yesterday that her Melissa, you know Melissa, Darling, she is your age, must be in some of your classes, well her Melissa is getting roses sent to her every Sunday. Mrs Morrings was saying her Melissa was taken out for dinner twice just last week Sweetie. Mrs Morrings was rather pleased with herself dare I say, and it would be so nice to tell her you have received flowers too Darling."

I rolled my eyes knowing that this shopping trip was only an excuse to talk about graduation. My mother continued talking without waiting for me to respond.

"Andreah's little girl Isobel, you know she is only six, she has been promised to the Pelkin's family. They have a little boy her age, quite a smart match for the families to make. All good business and very important for families like ours to make smart matches. There are many boys your age that would be smart choices Darling. We have tried inviting their families over for dinner parties but Sweetheart, you really must make more of an effort with your appearance. You are very pretty if only you would let me teach you how to use make-up and buy you some new dresses Darling."

I cut carrots with more and more violence as she rambled on. I could hear in her voice that she was nervous talking about arranged marriages with me. She knew how I felt and she knew I wouldn't agree to one even if she could find a family to arrange one with. I had finished with the vegetables and so turned back around to face her.

"Mum, like I said before, I'm busy on Saturday. I'm going to do stuff with Blake and quite frankly, I will be busy every day that you plan on getting me poked, prodded, plucked, or waxed by some stranger and force me to eat a limp salad with some of your friends and their air headed daughters."

Mum looked a little hurt but unsurprised at my words but still she fought for her cause. I had to admire her perseverance even if I despised her for it. This argument had been going on for months as she tried to push me into behaving more like the other girls. She wanted so badly to have a Daughter like Mrs Morrings' Melissa that I felt a little guilty soemtimes

I couldn't just stand still and let my life fly by.

"At least get a proposal out of Blake!" Mum was saying exasperatedly. "Get him to promise that on Graduation night he will propose to you. You have spent somuch time with him that no one else thinks you are available but I have never seen him make any signs that he will be proposing to you and I cannot rely on chance. Do not make me watch my only daughter go to the factories."

I stared at her for a moment before I turned and walked out of the kitchen, up the stairs and to my room to get changed for dinner. It was traditional customs to change into dress clothes for dinner as it was a formal family occasion. Dad took it very seriously. After I had changed and done my hair, I went back down stairs to help Mum set the table. She looked stunning in a new full length silk blue dress. It was obviously a very special dinner. I helped set up and then we both sat patiently at the table awaiting Dad's arrival home.

We sat in silence. Although I loved her a lot, I never really got on with my mum. She didn't understand my repulsion at learning the traditional ways of a woman. I wasn't interested in the cooking and the cleaning and I certainly didn't want to marry. She spent a lot of time, money and tears trying to make me interested in it all but I just wasn't. Our argument in the kitchen was proof we would never see eye to eye. We just didn't get along anymore: every conversation ended in an argument.

And so we sat, wanting to speak, but unable to talk.

It never used to be that way. Our family was well off enough that every weekend was an adventure. Throughout my childhood I was taken out often, just the three of us or sometimes with Blake too. We'd go to the movies, the museum, rock climbing, to the beach to look at the rock pools, kart racing- even mum would join in. My parents doted on me as I was an only child like Blake. But this last year, Mum started pressuring me and that's when the friction started. She stopped coming along to outings and disapproved of Dad taking me along on the adventures that she considered 'manly'. I was suddenly forbidden from rock climbing, kart racing, or even doing anything at the beach other than sun bathing. Instead I was to shop and focus on trying to make myself look as pretty as possible. Although she never went as far as to throw Blake out, she clearly wished I had more girl friends. I hated that she had suddenly done this to us. As both our personalities were water, we often clashed and the light around the house was tainted by dark blue spirits. I missed her.

The silence drew on.

My Water personality, Beatrice, was glaring at me from where she stood next to me. 'She's your mother, for crying out loud, tell her you think she looks beautiful!'

'I can't, it will be too awkward. She will expect me to keep up a conversation then and it will just end in an argument.'

'If a daughter can't talk to her mother then who can she talk to?'

'Well I do have Bl...'

'Blake, yes I know you tell him everything and he tells you everything but he's not a woman, he can't talk to you about woman things. Talk to your mother.'

'Oh ew Bea, I can't believe you just said that! I will not talk to her. I don't want to talk to her.'

'Fine, be like that, but don't blame me when you have no one to turn to!'

Bea and I glared at each other for a while longer. We were interrupted by the clock chiming nine pm. Dad was late, very late. Mum rose and went to the phone on the wall. She rang Dad's office in the centre of town. The woman at the desk told her that Dad had left over an hour ago. It only took fifteen minutes to get from the office to our home. Mum and I looked at each other. Our eyes said we both knew what had happened.

Missing.

My mother's Water personality had the wide eyed face that said it all. I didn't need to hear it to know what it was saying to Mum. My mum let out a whimper and ran upstairs with her personality flitting behind her. I was stunned.

'We have to find him,' I said to Bea in a strained voice.

'I know,' Bea said back in our mind.

Suddenly I jumped into action and raced upstairs. Bursting into my room I tore off my dress and my shoes and swapped them for a more sensible pair of jeans and a tee shirt. I laced on my pair of trainers and looked around for my school bag. It was lying against a leg of my desk. I grabbed it and turned it upside down, emptying it onto the floor. Books, pens, pencils, bits of lunch, a lipstick, hair brush, and sunglasses fell out. I replaced them with a map, my pocket knife, a torch and a blanket.

I raced back down to the kitchen and grabbed some food and a water bottle, stuffing it into my bag as I grabbed my coat off the hook at the front door and raced out of the house.

'What now?' Bea asked me.

'We go to Blake,' I thought, 'See if he wants to come and if he has any idea where Dad might be.'

Blake's house was just three streets down from where I lived. The air was still as the sun had only just set. I ran along the cobbled streets, trying not to fall in my haste as the big houses got smaller and smaller. Blake's house was closer to town and had a smaller garden than mine. It wasn't far between the two though and I was there before I had properly thought about what I was going to say. I knocked on the door and his mum answered.

"Hello Saffron," she said formally.

She looked down at me. I knew by her look that she did not approve of my outfit.

"It's a bit late to be calling and to be out alone, isn't it?"

Her Air personality glared at me with a wrinkled nose as if the sight of me made her smell something bad.

"Yes ma'am," I said apologetically. "I'm sorry to bother you but could I possibly talk to Blake please? It's somewhat an emergency."

"What's the matter?" Blake asked appearing behind his mother at the door. His mother looked at me with one last suffering glance and then left.

"Dad's gone missing," I said in a low voice. "He never came home from work."

Blake looked stunned. My dad had always wanted a son but instead they got me. After they had me the doctors told Mum that she couldn't have any more kids and so Dad was stuck with one daughter. As Blake's dad wasn't always the model father, my dad had sort of adopted Blake as a son. He approved of our friendship no end as it meant he got to do all the father-son activities after all. Because Dad liked Blake so much, I got along with him a lot better than Mum. I was determined to find him and Blake's face was slowly taking on a look of determination too.

"Stay here," he whispered. He darted up the stairs and was back again in two minutes also with a backpack.

"Let's go," he said. As he closed the front door he called out to the house,

"Going for a walk with Saffy."

The door slammed shut with a bang. Our personalities were waiting for us at the gate; deep colours of blue and green as our determination to find my father grew stronger.

Chapter Three

Into the Shadows

We ran.

The streets were deserted as it came close to ten o'clock. As we neared the shops we came across Authority Guards patrolling the area. We skidded to a stop and crouched in the shadows. Although they were supposed to be the good guys, the Guards were 'act first think later' kind of people and any one out this late, especially two kids, were going to be seen as suspicious. Not wanting to be caught and stopped from searching for my dad, we lurked in the shadows, watching their movements and waiting for an opportunity. We were on the street that had my dad's office on it. On this street were twelve armed Guards with their personalities, all of them Fire, three dogs and a truck with who knows what inside.

"I need to get inside Dad's office," I said to Blake. "That was the last time someone saw him. He might have left something behind that could tell us where he went."

I looked back at the street. Although it was dark, the Guards had set up sweeping spot lights. Their red uniforms flashed every time the light hit them and their personalities were flitting around, casting more shadows. It reminded me of pools of blood. I swallowed. Dad's office was the other end of the street. How on earth were we to get there?

"Looks like we are going roof jumping," Blake said with a smile as if to answer my question. I stared at him and a smile crept up my face too. He took off his bag and unzipped it. Inside were an assortment of tools and a long piece of rope. He grinned at my shocked expression.

"I came prepared."

"Clearly," I muttered, helping him arrange the rope. We tied ourselves to each end.

"Ready?" I asked him.

"Race you," he grinned at me. A flicker of guilt ran through me as I realised I was about to do an activity that Mum would most definitely disapprove of. It sent a rush through me that made me grin back at Blake, a childish glint in my eye as the competition built in both of us. Blake and mine's friendship was built on our ability to know what the other was thinking and this made for great team work.

Our personalities watched from the roof as we climbed. Despite the constant adventures as a child, I was never keen on heights. Although this building wasn't that tall, I was still coated in a layer of sweat that had nothing to do with the exertion of the climb. My fear was small enough that Bea was only a slight shade clearer than normal as she waited for me. Standing next to her, Caspar seemed greener than ever Bea's colour. Blake was showing off that he'd never been afraid to climb. It didn't take us long to scale the building as it was badly secured and the window ledges were wide. Once on top it was clear to see how far we had to go until we reached Dad's office. We untied ourselves and I put the rope back in Blake's bag.

Then we ran. The buildings in our town were built fairly close together and with a run up, it is possible to jump from one building to another almost with ease. We were both fast and incredibly competitive. Without realising, this had become almost fun and all fear of the height we were jumping at was forgotten as I pushed myself harder and harder. Panting and sweating we reached the rooftop of Dad's office. The door to the roof was locked but Blake soon had it open with one of his tools.

This was something I admired of him. His father had taught him some skills that were rather unsavoury that my dad had never taught me. Unlocking a door without a key was practically magic to me and yet Blake managed it with ease. Unlocked, the door swung open and we crept down the stairs to the second floor. Sneaking down the hallway we passed door after door until we reached his office.

Dad's office was a rather small room with a desk, a chair, a bookcase, a small sofa, and a large window. From this window you could see right out across town, all the way to the meadow and the woods beyond. Behind his desk was a beautiful painting of a lion walking away from the sunset.

When I used to visit Dad at the office as a child, this painting would scare me because the light made the lion's mane look like it was on fire. The colours were like nothing I had ever seen at any of the museums we used to visit and it captivated my attention every time I walked into the room. I couldn't stop staring at it. It was one of those paintings where the eyes seem to follow you across the room and I suddenly had the horrible feeling that we were being watched.

We crept stealthily around the office. Using little flash lights from

Blake's bag, we looked for any clues as to when he was taken. I sat in his chair behind the desk and looked through the draws. A piece of paper caught my eye. It was a page ripped out from a book. On it was a vast amount of philosophical writing and someone, it must have been Dad, had circled one part of it;

"For we are nothing without our personalities, and without us they are also nothing.

We are zombie like in function without them, a mere corpse.

The darkness of nothingness is impossible to ignore or forget

yet a champion must rise before all succumb to the fate of control."

Scrawled in the margins someone had written, '*here they come*'. I gasped and showed Blake.

"He knew what was going on," I said quietly. "He knew where all the missing people were going and now they've taken him too."

"But where?" Blake wondered, reading the piece of paper again. I looked up and out the window into the black of the night.

"The woods," I murmured.

We both looked out of the window. From here we could see over the tops of the trees all the way into the distance but the view never changed; just more trees. I could see where the wood got thicker from this height but not where it ended the other side. We had to go there, I knew it. All those times we had spent sitting in the meadow just a stone's throw away from all the bad things that had happened in the town. I wondered just where in the bad things that had been happening in the town. I wondered just where in the wood we would end up and how we would find where we needed to go. We had never spent much time in the woods. There was another patch of woodland on the other side of town that had a bike track and hiking trails that everyone used, but this wood was a reserve for wild animals and so not many people ever ventured in. Sometimes a group of us would get together on a Friday night and see how far we could go in but it was never far before someone got spooked. It was the wood for all the fairytales: Red Riding Hood's wood, Hansel and Gretel's wood, Jack's wood, the wood of monsters and witches, of moonlight and shadows: as if you could go in and find yourself in a giant's castle in the sky or a house made of cakes. A bright light shone through the window and we dropped to the ground.

"We need to get out of here," Blake whispered urgently.

At that moment the floor started vibrating and hundreds of heavy boots could be heard running up the stairs of the building we were in. From the window we could see the Authority Guards' personalities all staying outside on patrol and yet there was still more Authority Guards swarming into the office.

'Now what?!' Beatrice said in my head.

"We have to get out of here! Now!" I said in a panicked voice. Blake was looking around the room for places to hide, the desk? No that was too obvious. He looked towards the window.

"We could jump?" he said to me desperately.

"The smashed glass would draw too much attention to us, we'd never get away!" I was terrified that we would be caught and shot if we didn't move soon.

We were looking around the room frantically trying to find a way out when I caught sight of the painting of the lion. I stared into its face and saw that its eyes were looking up at the ceiling. I looked where it was looking and saw the vent. I nudged Blake and pointed. He looked and nodded. We crawled over until we were directly under it. I climbed onto Blake's shoulders and opened the vent. As the sound of heavy boots burst into the hallway I scrambled up into the space in the ceiling. I reached down and grabbed Blake's hands. Heaving, I helped him pull himself up into the vent with me. Casper and Bea flitted in behind him before I replaced the vent guard just as men came storming into the office. We held our breath, waiting for them to leave. They did a sweep of the room and declared it clear. They moved out of the room and towards the stairs to check the next floor.

We began to crawl along through the vent system. It was a maze of metal and we had to be very quiet, one small noise could bring the entire force on us. After a few minutes, we found ourselves against an outside wall. I peered through the vent guard. We were only one storey up now. I looked over my shoulder at Blake.

"We might as well jump," I said.

He nodded and I opened up the guard. Carefully I lowered myself out and then dropped to the ground. I looked around quickly and got out of the way of Blake who fell beside me. We peered around and started running alongside the building, sticking to the shadows. We turned the corner and ducked into the shadows to avoid the search light sweeping the streets. From here we could see the woods but to get there we would have to cross the meadow where there was no cover. Throwing caution to the wind, we ran. In our head Beatrice screamed. Simultaneously there was a shout from behind us. Suddenly we were in a flood of light. We froze like a deer in headlights. There was a shout and then bullets were whizzing through the air towards us.

"Run!" I shouted.

We sprinted as fast as we could towards the safety of the trees. Bullets were ricocheting off surroundings and I could feel the wind rush past me as bullets flew so close to us but none hit us as we ducked through the trees.

We kept running as it got darker and darker in the woods. Soon everything was quiet except our pounding feet and our heavy breathing.

"That," Blake breathed, "was too close for comfort."

"And they're supposed to be on our side," I gasped. I wasn't hit but I could feel the stabbing of a stitch in my side.

"You're not hit are you?"

"No, I'm fine."

'What do we do now?' Beatrice thought.

I looked around us. We were surrounded by trees. Deep in the woods it was difficult to see past the gloom. The wind rustled the trees and set my arms alight with goose bumps.

"Should...have...brought...water," Blake panted. We took off our backpacks and sat down against a tree. I opened mine up and handed him the water bottle.

"I came prepared," I said, grinning cheekily up at him.

"Clearly," Blake muttered back.

We sat down to drink. While I had my backpack open, I got out the torch as it really was getting darker. There was a howl and a rustle of leaves somewhere behind Blake. We stopped moving and listened. There were things running through the trees around us. Our heads spun as we searched the shadows of the trees for the source of the noise. The rustling got louder from the lighter area of the wood. We picked up our stuff and ran. We crashed through the undergrowth like bulls in a china shop. All the while Bea was screaming mutely in our head. We stormed past trees, over dead branches, forcing a path away from our pursuers. Bea and Casper led the way, leaving a slight glow long enough for us to follow their path.

No matter how fast we ran they seemed to be right behind us. I couldn't take it any longer. Too puffed to run, I stopped to fight. Switching on the torch, I shined it into the shadows. The minute the light came on there was a whine and a massive shadow of a beast was illuminated against the trees. The torch shook in my hands as the shadow grew larger and larger. We inched back until a tree blocked our path. Blake drew a knife from his bag and stood in front of me. The snarling shadow of a beast was almost upon us. My hand was shaking so hard that I almost dropped the torch. Casper and Bea stood on our flanks worriedly looking on.

From where the shadow was coming from, there were sounds of something fast crashing though the bushes. Suddenly, mid-snarl, the creature vanished. I dropped the torch and sank to the ground behind Blake. He didn't turn around but kept searching the dark for the predator. A faint glow of light was coming towards us from the same place as the beast had been. A rustling sound was coming from where the beast had vanished.

I peered through the gloom as a boy emerged from the trees. He was dirty, disheveled and something about him was wrong. There was something unbalanced about him that I couldn't quite place, as if he was strangely deformed.

"Who are you?" Blake stepped forward cautiously to stand beside me in front of this strange new boy. The boy looked fleetingly from Blake to me and back but didn't answer the question.

Blake stepped forward threateningly. "I asked you a question. Now answer me!"

I got up and stepped forward towards the boy cautiously and slowly, hoping not to frighten him. He looked straight at me with panicked eyes.

"What is your name?" I asked him softly. I offered him my water bottle and he drank deeply from it. When he had quenched his thirst he handed me back the water bottle and with a more controlled expression, finally answered our question.

"My name," he said somewhat calmly, "is Sebastian."

"Will you tell us your story? Why are you here in the woods?" I asked him. He looked only at me now.

"It is rather a long story."

"We can't go any further tonight," Blake interrupted abruptly. "You might as well tell us who you are." He paused for a moment and said to me, "May I speak to you a moment in private?"

We moved away from Sebastian and whispered to each other. "Do you think we should trust this guy? I don't like him."

I looked at Blake.

"Don't you think we should wait until we've heard his story before we pass judgment? Besides, he might know something."

"Exactly," Blake whispered back. "What if he's one of the rebels?"

I thought about this for a moment.

"Blake, he looked so scared when he found us. I think we should hear his story and figure out if we can use any of the information he gives us. And I think we should offer for him to stay with us if he wants to."

Blake looked at me with an unfathomable expression then lifted an eyebrow.

"What happened to not passing judgment yet?"

His tone was sarcastic and I didn't appreciate it. My answering tone therefore, was louder than it should have been for our private conversation.

"Does he really look dangerous to you Blake?"

"I'm not here to hurt you," Sebastian called through the trees where we'd left him. I nodded at Blake and stalked back through to the clearing.

"Ok," I said, sitting down on the clearing floor. "Tell us your story."

Chapter Four

Sebastian

"If you keep going through the woods that way," Sebastian started speaking only to me and unnecessarily pointing to the left where there was such a thick growth of plants that we couldn't see any way, "you come to a ridge of mountains. The other side of the mountains is the town that I am from.

"I am nineteen years old now but I haven't been home in ten years. When I was nine, people started going missing from our town. We thought at first that the woodland wolves had started attacking the village but soon people were going missing so frequently that it couldn't have been any animal. Then one day the Authority Guards turned up to help protect the few of us that were left. By this point at least half the village was missing. I lost my father first. My mother was so upset she didn't leave the house after that. I think that is what probably kept her safe. My brother had died as a baby and I had no other siblings so it was up to me to look after my mother. Our neighbours were very kind and made sure we had enough to eat- as much as they could- but my mother was never the same again.

"I think she went a little crazy. I loved my mother but she was always fragile. My father adored her. he would come home early from work sometimes and we would sit in the kitchen, mother cooking, father playing his guitar, all of us singing and laughing the evening away. She had the sweetest voice in the village; everyone yearned to hear her sing. When father didn't come home at all that day I thought mother was going to be fine. She ever so calmly walked up to the front door that night and bolted it shut like my father used to do every night at the same time. Without a word she went to bed. Things went on normally enough until winter came. It was so very cold and the Authority Guards were rationing everything. There was nothing left for the fire. One night it was so cold I became sick. I remember my mother crossing the room to where father's guitar was sitting, picking it up and smashing it to pieces. She lit a fire using his guitar. That fire kept me alive that night and for every night since then but it broke my mother. As soon as I was well again my mother took to her bed and never came out again. I took food up to her and she ate it vacantly. I realised that by being sick, I had broken my mother and I desperately tried to make her better but as a nine year old boy, there was not a lot I could do other than feed her and keep her safe from the Authority Guards.

"It soon became clear that the Authority Guards didn't really see the need in protecting us from whatever was going on. They looted shops, attacked the men without reasons, and forced themselves on the girls that were left. By this point most of us were just waiting to die, or whatever was happening to all the missing people. It seemed our fates were sealed. The village gates had been closed for months, no one was allowed in or out. The people were starving, prisoners in their own homes. There were a few people that tried to fight the Authority Guards, to rebel against our so called protectors.

“Those who did fight against their regimes were punished. We often had to stand on ceremony and watch a public whipping. The ones who caused a lot of trouble simply disappeared in the night never to be seen again. I think we were supposed to believe they had been taken by whoever was stealing people, but it was always a little too convenient and everyone knew the Guards were quietly killing rule breakers.

“One night during the winter holidays I had gone for a walk. There was a part of the village wall I found easy to climb over so I would often escape for a while. I had explored around the village often with the other boys but there were only a few of us left now. Many of the boys were more interested in playing guard than explorer and I was scared they would tell someone I was sneaking off so I didn’t tell anyone when I went.

“This night I was out later than I was supposed to be. There was a hill I liked to visit where you could see the whole village and way beyond that. From there I saw the Authority Guards raiding a pub. Their yells were carried to me on the wind. I watched as they lit a bonfire. I was entranced by its colours; it had been a while since we had been able to light a fire. I found out later that they had ransacked houses for furniture to burn.

“As the night grew on, the Authority Guards got more and more drunk. I knew that I should be home, that it was way past curfew. I knew my mother would be worrying but I was too scared to try to get home. I would have had to pass the Guards and I was just too scared to move. I decided to wait until they passed out drunk before trying to go home.

“So I settled down in the cold, waiting for the Guards to sleep. But they didn’t. I sat and watched as they ran through the houses where people still lived, watched as they rounded them up in the town square. I watched two Guards go into my house and ice ran down my spine thinking of my weak mother lying in bed. A few moments later I watched them drag my mother out of the house by her arms, her legs dragging behind her. I was too far away to see but I knew she wouldn't be wearing any shoes. I was too far away to hear but I knew she would be singing softly under her breath, the last song we had heard my father play before he went missing, just as she had been ever since I was sick. I saw them take out their guns and I felt the gun fire echo through my body. The image of my mother's fragile body collapsing to the ground amongst all the other villagers still haunts me. I thought now I would be able to go and tend to my mother's body. My thoughts wondered wildly around burying her in the woods where she would always be free. But the Guards weren't done yet. They began digging in the village square. It took them all night to dig a big enough and deep enough hole but once they were done they roughly shoved all the bodies into it, covered it back up with soil and left."

Sebastian broke off and stared out into the trees. He seemed to be thinking of how to continue his story. I couldn't bare it.

"Please, don't tell us anymore." My voice was choked from being quiet for so long and the thought of all those people dying. "People are going missing in our town too. My dad has gone. The Authority Guards they arrived just a few days ago to protect the rest of us from the rebel's attacks. Our friends. Our family. I couldn't bear it."

"I lost everyone that night," Sebastian said quietly but he said no more after that. We sat in silence for a while. Sebastian was clearly thinking over what I had said and he quickly broke the silence. "We never knew the rebels were behind it. Is that what The Authority is telling people?"

"Yes. The rebels are taking people to build an army! They are going to start a war. That is why the Authority Guards have been stationed at our town, to protect us. How could they attack the very people they are there to save? I don't understand who would allow them to behave that way. Don't they have to follow orders? If they just killed everyone they were supposed to protect what are they supposed to do afterwards, just move onto the next town? It's too much!"

"I suppose they just grew tired," Sebastian said quietly.

He looked down and his face was shadowed, hiding his expression from me. Blake shifted position, rustling the leaves under him. From the corner of my eye I saw him stand up. He folded his arms across his chest and looked down at where Sebastian was sitting.

Blake loomed over Sebastian and in the dark he looked quite sinister. I spoke from where I sat on the floor.

"Tired of protecting people? It is their job! How do you wake up one morning and decide that you're bored of keeping people alive?"

Blake completely ignored me and asked a different question.

"So what have you been doing for the past ten years?"

I thought his tone was rather suspicious. It was abrupt and unnecessarily angry so I glared at him. he didn't seem to get the point of

I thought his tone was rather suspicious. It was abrupt and unnecessarily angry so I glared at him. He didn't seem to get the point of anything that we'd just talked

about. Something about Sebastian made Blake uneasy and I could see him fighting to remain in control of the situation. Casper was flanking Blake facing Sebastian. They both had their backs to me so I couldn't see their faces but I could see Sebastian through their legs. His face, illuminated by Casper's glow, was unaffected by Blake's show of aggression. Sebastian smiled slightly at the ground then looked up into Blake's eyes and calmly replied.

"Trying to find out where all the missing people are and how to save them," he said. "I know where they are being kept but I don't know what to do."

I looked at Blake excitedly. He turned around to face me as I spoke.

"Where are they being kept?"

"In a castle through the other side of the woods," Sebastian said, pointing through the trees. He was speaking only to me again, keeping his eyes on my face and paying no attention to Blake. I could see that this was frustrating Blake a little but I couldn't worry about that now.

"Can you take us there?" I demanded.

"Of course," Sebastian said. "Although I'm not sure what you can do about it."

He got to his feet and looked down at me where I was sitting cross legged on the ground. My earlier label of him as a boy was clearly wrong.

As he had put it right in his story, he was nineteen, a year older than me and Blake. This knowledge changed the way I looked at him. Now that he had sat for a while and had something to drink, the wild look had left his face. He was clearly calmer and this left me more confident in looking at the rest of him. His clothes were dirty which was expected of someone on the run. He was tall and slim with clear bulges of muscle on his arms. He looked strong despite his story of sadness. I blushed as my eyes scanned back to his face. He had been watching me looking over him. Suddenly I realised why he was still looking at me: he was waiting for me to reply. He distracted me very easily I noticed. But I couldn't let him distract me too much. I had things I had to do.

"I have to save my dad."

I finally spoke out loud and stood up like the boys. If there was any chance that Sebastian was right and that the castle was where the people were being kept, then I had to go there. It was a start; even if Dad wasn't there it was better than hiking aimlessly through the woods.

"Not tonight," Blake said turning his back on me. "Right now, we need to sleep. Casper and Bea can keep watch."

He started picking up sticks of different sizes and arranging them ready to light. The fire glowed in the clearing and the boys sat back down again near it, fending off the chill that had come with the darkness. I stood for a moment longer, impatient.

I knew it was the best idea but I was still rattled at Blake for suggesting sleep when we had just found a lead to getting my dad back. I lay down and stared at the canopy of trees above me. As the night grew

grew darker and Sebastian's story continued, the fire lit up our faces and fought the cold in the dark. Now that we were settling down for the night I was glad of the warm fire. I got cold far too easily, a fact well known to Blake. I suspected this was his reasoning to building a fire: he wouldn't be cold tonight even without the fire. It was a warm night for this time of year but still I shivered and moved closer to the flames. I watched the smoke drift lazily up to dance among the stars.

'What do you think about Sebastian?' I asked Bea silently. 'He's been through so much.'

'Yes but can we trust him?'

'I'm not sure. There's something....' She trailed off unable to finish her sentence.

'I know what you mcan. I gucss wc'll just havc to wait and scc.'

***

That night I dreamed.

Saffy sat at a table looking across at her mother. Her mother was glaring back. The room was silent. Looking down at her plate she saw that it was playing a video like some sort of television. She looked up at her parents in shock and still they said nothing. Saffy leaned in closer to watch what was happening on her plate. As she focused on the plate the dream took her to a new dimension. Looking up and around her she saw that she was in a wood but the wood was on fire. Everywhere around her were animals fleeing from the flames.

Aware that this was a dream in the strange way I sometimes was, I looked around at the blazing trees.

A loud snap caused Saffy to look around.

With a slow muffled interest that often accompanies dreams I stepped away from the falling burning branch.

The branch misses her but the flames behind her are too close and singe her back.

I feel the pain.

It is getting hotter and hotter. Looking around Saffy knows she is trapped. The flames are everywhere and getting closer to her every second. It is getting harder for Saffy to breathe. The flames lick the trees around her, travelling along branches that hang just feet away from where she stands. The heat is intense but Saffy is cold.

In her hands she holds the dinner plate and in the dinner plate she sees herself looking back at her, screaming.

Back at the table Saffy watches herself burn while her parents look on in disgust at her screams. Saffy cannot feel herself burning but she screams along with herself as she burns inside the plate. It hurts but the pain is disjointed as Saffy sits at the dining table screaming at her plate. Her parents have been quietly eating all this time, ignoring their daughter.

"You will burn Saffron." Her father tells her without even looking up from his plateful of food. "You will feel the blistering pain of heat on your skin and you will burn."

With a jolt I awoke.

Shaking from the cold and sweating from the dream I look around me. The embers of our fire were still glowing, pulsing. On one side of me Sebastian was snoring softly with a slight frown on his face. Blake was quiet the other side of me. I rearranged the blanket I had brought with me so that it was covering all three of us again. Blake stirred and shifted. I couldn't tell if he was awake or not but I stayed quiet and he didn't say anything. A glow caught my eye and I spun my head around but it was only Casper staring at me intently. His gaze was not friendly and as my eyes drooped shut in sleep again I could have sworn I saw his eyes glint red.

As I fell once more into dreamland, I watched Bea fly silently over the trees, over where we slept, keeping an eye out above while Casper watched from the ground. At that moment I thought I realized what was wrong with Sebastian but before the thought had formed completely in my head, I was asleep.

In the morning I will remember nothing.

Chapter Five

The Heart Pendant

The next morning I awoke to Blake shaking me. It was dawn and everything was soaked in the grey colour of the time just before morning really began. At some point in the night I had cocooned myself in the blanket I had brought with me. I felt a pang of guilt that the boys had not tried to share it.

"Were you not cold?" I asked as I stuffed the blanket back into my bag.

"I wouldn't have slept well anyway," Blake replied. I looked around the clearing.

"Where's Sebastian?" I looked suspiciously at Blake.

"He walked off that way," Blake said pointing into the trees. Then seeing my expression he held his hands up in defense. "Hey don't look at me like that; he went on his own free will without saying anything. Maybe he doesn't want to help you."

"Or maybe he just went to find some food for breakfast." Sebastian walked through the trees with arms full of fruit. "I thought we could take some with us in your back packs."

"Thanks," I said, smiling at him and walking over to take an apple. I bit down on it and crisp cold juice flowed into my mouth. I took another apple from Sebastian and threw it at Blake. He caught the apple with one hand and put it straight into his backpack without even looking at Sebastian.

“We should start looking for your dad, don’t you think so Saf?”

I looked down, a lump in my throat, unable to swallow the apple in my mouth. Of course I was worried about my father and I was in a hurry to find him but I didn’t think that having an apple would slow me down that much, especially when Blake had made us camp over night. I was angry at him for being a jerk. He made me feel bad about something as simple as food. I glared at Blake, the apple hanging limply in my hand.

“It’s this way,” Sebastian said quietly, turning around and starting to walk into the trees. Blake strode after him. I spat out my mouthful of apple which now tasted like dirt, ran over to my backpack and stuffed the other apples in it. Hurriedly zipping it up I ran to catch up with the boys.

Bea was flitting through the trees next to me but she didn’t talk to me. I could feel her compassion and mutual guilt over Blake’s mood today and it made me feel worse. Up ahead I could see the boys and Casper walking through the trees. I stopped and watched them walk away from me. Both boys were similar in build but looked very different. Blake’s dark messy hair contrasted brilliantly against Sebastian’s neat blond hair. Blake’s personality was Earth. He looked strong and intimidating. He moved with purpose looking in every direction, constantly wary of the woods and the dangers he knew lay ahead of us. Even from this distance I could see him analysing every potential threat. Caspar must have said something to Blake in their head as Blake turned around at that moment to see me standing still so far away.

Blake ran back to where I was standing. Bea was circling me with a confused look on her face as she tried to make sense of the mixed emotions in our head. He reached us with a worried look on his face.

"What's wrong?" he asked.

He looked straight into my eyes and I could see the fear and concern in them. He looked around for the danger he thought I was in. But there was none. Confused, he looked back at me, waiting for an explanation. Instinct told me it was my turn to talk so I forced a smile and looked right into Blake's dark brown eyes.

"Nothing is wrong; it just took me a little longer to grab my stuff than you two." Relief flooded unmasked across his face as he stared unnervingly into my eyes.

"I'm sorry, we should have waited. Come on."

We started walking towards where Sebastian was waiting for us. We walked in silence but in our head, Bea and I were loudly discussing everything.

'What was that?' Bea demanded. 'I'm supposed to understand every feeling and thought you have but that was something else! Do you care to explain what went down while you were looking at those two together?'

'I'm sorry I made you nervous but I think you couldn't understand how I was feeling because I didn't understand it myself.'

'One minute you were fine and then you were looking at the boys. I knew that first feeling, it is the same feeling you have always felt when you look at Blake. I feel it every time your heart skips a beat.'

'Oh, shut up. I don't feel anything for Blake.'

'You do too but that's not the point. When you started looking at Sebastian, I could sense something else, something stronger. You already really like him, even though you don't know anything about him, but there is something that I'm uneasy about with him. I just don't know what.'

'I know. I feel your uneasiness but maybe it's just that we don't know him.

'Maybe... but I want to talk about the biggest mess of feelings that swamped you back then. You stopped paying attention to Sebastian and moved on to Casper. And that surprised me the most. Why are you afraid of Casper?'

'I'm not.

'You are. I felt it; fear so deep that it left you unable to continue walking. That is what caused you to stop. Fear. Fear of the most intense value, the kind that makes me become almost transparent in form and leaves you unable to move even a muscle. Further than a panic over heights or bugs or any other irrational flutter. But I don't understand it, you are not afraid of Blake, so why should you fear his personality, they are one.'

Our conversation was interrupted by Sebastian. He was at the front of our line, leading the way. We had travelled all day. Usually on our hikes, Blake and I would talk non-stop and if we got tired of that or ran out of pointless things to say, we would sing our way through the trees. This didn't happen often as we almost always had something to say but the songs would make the hike more fun and everyone we passed would not stop smiling. But now we didn't sing. We didn't even talk and so the walk went on for hours. It was made worse for me by being trapped in my head with Bea. The entire walk she had been highlighting my fears. Fear of Casper, fear of losing my dad, fear of where we were. I was just beginning to get thirsty when I started to hear running water to our left. We passed through the thinning trees and found Sebastian had led us to a stream. He sat down on a rock and looked up at us where we stood.

"You can refill your water bottle here. The water is clean and you'll need more water for the rest of the day."

While I filled my water bottle, Sebastian stayed on the rock, further away from the water. Blake stayed with his bag and opened it.

"We should eat here while we still have daylight, we shouldn't let ourselves get too hungry. I didn't bring any food, did you?"

He turned to where I was paddling in the cool water.

"I nicked a loaf of bread from the kitchen that was supposed to be with dinner but that was all. I should have brought more."

Blake turned back to his bag and pulled out a ball of plastic looking thin wire and a small hammer.

"There's fish in that stream. I could see them in the deeper part just further in. We can catch them if I make some basic hand lines."

While he was talking, Blake was unravelling the ball of wire.

"What is that?" I asked him nodding to his hands.

"It is nylon. It will work as the fishing line."

He took hold of his hammer and unscrewed the head from the handle.

"I'm going to use this as the weight to keep tension in the line. Now for the bait."

He looked around then walked over to Sebastian.

"Stand up."

Confused, Sebastian stood up and Blake lifted the rock that Sebastian had been sitting on. Crawling all over it were black beetles. I involuntarily screeched and backed up. He paled and turned to Sebastian.

"Can you please get those for me?"

Sebastian looked at Blake's pale face then at mine and picked up a few of the biggest put them in a pot that Blake had grabbed from his backpack, and turned to face us again. Both of us were gaining the colour back in our faces although I noticed Casper was still a lime green instead of his usual brightness. Blake rummaged through his pack looking lost.

"I can't find the hook. I can't fish without the hook and I don't have anything to make one out of."

"What could you make one out of if you had it?" Sebastian asked. He had a look of awe on his face, clearly impressed with Blake's ability to use his surroundings.

"I need a piece of metal that I can bend to a hook."

There was silence as we all thought about what we had with us.

"How about this?" Sebastian asked, holding up a stick. Blake looked at it but quickly dismissed it.

"It isn't heavy enough or robust enough. It just wouldn't work at all."

"No need to be so blunt," Sebastian muttered. "I was only trying to help."

"Well then what about a rock?" I asked Blake, distracting him from Sebastian's comment. Blake shook his head.

"That wouldn't work either, they are blunt so wouldn't catch anything. It needs to be sharp so that I can put a beetle on it for the fish to eat but it also has to be hooked enough to catch hold of the fish so it can't swim away."

"Do you have anything in your backpack that could be used?" Sebastian asked me.

"I don't think so," I replied, looking inside my bag.

"Well, it is hopeless without a hook. I can't catch any fish without one," Blake sighed and sat down on a rock.

Looking around me I automatically reached for my necklace. I always splayed with it while thinking hard and this time it immediately gave me the answer. I quickly unlatched it from around my neck. It was a silver necklace with a large hollow heart

on it. It was plain and simple but I liked it that way. It was cheap and was starting to tarnish as the metal could be seen through the silver coating. I threw it over to Blake.

"Will this work?"Blake looked it over and tested its durability, bending it a little.

"It'll have to do."

He smiled up at me and a look came across his face.

"I'm sorry about your necklace, I promise to get you another. The heart I give you won't tarnish or break."

He said this as he snapped the necklace in half and created two perfect halves of a heart. He looked around for a rough rock and, once he had found one, filed the broken heart to a point. After attaching it to the line above the weight he gingerly took his pot of beetles and stabbed one onto the end. He waded out to where there was a tall rock that marked the beginning of the deeper water. He stood on that and threw his line into the deeper pool. Turning back to us he called over to Sebastian.

"Use the other half of the necklace and make your own line with the rest of the nylon. If you fish too we'll eat quicker."

"I can't," Sebastian called back.

"Sure you can, you just watched me do it and I can instruct you from here." Sebastian looked uncomfortable.

"No," he said quietly. "I can't fish. I'm afraid of water. I can't swim and I don't like going in it."

Blake looked incredulously at Sebastian then without a word turned back to his fishing. Sebastian blushed and looked down. Uncomfortable I went over to my back pack and pulled out a map.

"Why don't you look for some wood for a fire while Blake fishes?" I said in what I hoped was a kind yet unpatronising tone. Without a word Sebastian stood and walked off back into the woods.

'Watch over him,' I said to Bea in our head. From the corner of my eye I saw her emerge from the stream and follow Sebastian.

"Do you have to be so cruel to him?" I said to Blake.

"Cruel to whom?" he asked from the stream.

"Sebastian."

I looked at him while gesturing back into the woods where Sebastian had gone to get firewood. As I watched, Blake caught a fish and pulled it in on his make shift line.

"I'm not cruel to him I just don't like him. He knows I don't like him so why do I have to pretend to be nice?"

The harshness in his voice made me flinch. Most of the time Blake was a really nice guy, especially when he was away from his other friends, but sometimes he was a real jerk.

"Do it for me Blake. Be nice to him for me. Or if you can't do that, do it for my father. Sebastian says he can lead us to him. Don't give him a reason to stop. He's our only hope of getting Dad back. Remember that next time you choose to be horrid."

Blake looked abashed as he brought the fish he had caught up onto the bank where I was sitting. He got out his knife and gutted the fish in the shallow water of the stream. I continued looking over the map figuring out where we were. The stream was big enough to be on the map, I just had to decide where along the stream we were. I frowned as I saw something that confused me.

"Hey Blake," I called over to him. "We seem to be headed off the map."

"What do you mean?" he called back.

"I mean that I don't know where we are going. The map finishes with the woods and no one has ever talked of anything being beyond them in this direction."

“You think it is a trap? How do we even know we can trust Sebastian?”

I frowned again.

“That was not where I was going with this conversation Blake, you know I trust him. My point is if we don’t know where we are going, how are we supposed to get back again?”

Chapter Six

Sink or Swim

We sat around the fire that Sebastian had built and ate the fish Blake had caught and cooked with the bread I had bought with me from home. We were lucky enough to be eating real food even though we had minimal resources. As I had missed dinner the night before with my parents, I was very hungry. The boys were evidently very hungry too as there was not a lot of conversation going on as we ate our fish.

Blake had caught five fish so we had enough to eat. Between the three of us we ate four of the catch. The last fish I wrapped in some big leaves to put in my bag for later. As Blake was eating he started asking Sebastian questions about where we were headed.

"I already told you about the castle outside of the woods," Sebastian said. A little exasperation coloured his voice.

"Is that really all you can tell us? How close did you get to the castle?"

"Close enough to know that's where all the missing people are. You're just going to have to trust me. Can you do that?" Sebastian replied to Blake's question and asked his own. I interjected before Blake could reply.

"Yes."

After we had finished eating and had cleaned up in the stream I topped up my water bottle. I now had apples, slightly stale bread, and some left over fish in my back pack for us to snack on along with a full bottle of fresh water. We continued on, following the water downstream. The stream was getting wider and deeper as we walked. The boys stayed closer to the line of trees away from the water. Eventually we came to a make shift bridge. There were large boulders in the water and someone before us had found logs to walk along between them. The water was clear and gentle but deep. I watched as leaves from the trees floated along past rocks and swirled with the current. The sun shattered on the water's surface and made the slick wet rocks glisten like gems. The trees cast shadows onto the deeper parts of the river where the waters were not flowing as fast. As a breeze drifted across the water, more leaves fell from the trees. The whole atmosphere was serene and I breathed in its tranquillity. Blake looked suspiciously at the bridge, determining its strength. Casper was looking around with squinted eyes. Obviously neither of them felt as calm as I did looking at the water.

"Someone has been this way before. Why else would there be this bridge? The question is why? Where was this person going? Who was it?"

There was a pause as we processed all of these questions then Sebastian stepped forward.

"Yes," Sebastian replied.

"Someone has been this way before. Me. I built this. The only other option was to swim across and well, you know how much I like to swim."

He gave a sheepish grin and I saw his eyes twinkle.

"It's quite safe. Here, I'll go first. Saffy take my hand."

I walked towards Sebastian who was still smiling at me and put my hand in his.

"Watch your step; it can be a bit slippery."

We wobbled along the logs to each boulder, Blake behind us. The water seemed to move a lot faster now that we were above it. What once seemed like a calm body of water, now felt like a dangerous one. The water seemed to crash upon the rocks instead of flowing around them. Droplets splashed up onto our feet as if daring us to make a wrong move. I squeezed Sebastian's hand as I over balanced and he grabbed my waist to steady me.

"I've got you," he breathed in my ear.

"Are you alright Saffy?" Blake called from behind us. I was still staring at Sebastian when I called back.

"Yes. Yes, I'm fine."

I was very aware of Sebastian's hand on my waist. It was warm and the heat was spreading up my spine into my cheeks. He grinned at my blush and that sent my tummy into spirals of delight.

"Good. Then let's keep moving shall we?" Blake replied pointedly.

Sebastian let go of my waist but kept hold of my hand as we finished crossing the water. With a final jump we made it to a rocky bank the other side of the stream. I let go of Sebastian' hand and walked to the edge of the tress. There in the shade was a fallen tree. I sat down on it and opened my back pack, getting out the food. There was no point in rationing food that would just go off in my backpack so we finished off the bread and fish. Deciding there would probably be other fruit trees along the way, I handed out the apples too. I could feel Bea's disappointment in our head but she didn't say anything and neither did I. The sun was starting to set and a suggestion was made for us to camp on the bank tonight.

"I'll go and get some firewood," Blake said in a grumpy tone.

I looked at Bea in an exasperated way. She gave me a disapproving look, nodded, and followed Blake into the woods. I walked over to where Sebastian was sitting, eating an apple.

"Hey," I said softly. "I never, you know, said thank you for saving me before."

I awkwardly looked at my feet and twisted my fingers.

"Well I couldn't have you falling in could I?" he said back, grinning.

"If you had bumped your head on those rocks we really could have been in trouble and I might have never seen you blush again."

"But still," I said, looking down at where he sat in front of me, "thank you."

"It was a good excuse to hold you," he replied, grinning up at me. He took another bite of his apple and munched, his eyes twinkling. "You're very nice to hold. You fit perfectly in my hands."

"Yeah, well, don't get used to it," I spluttered. I attempted to sound nonchalant and cutting but I wasn't sure that I had pulled it off.

"Too late, I already am."

As if on cue I felt the blood rise in my cheeks and I laughed nervously and sat down next to him.

"You are beautiful Saffron," Sebastian whispered quietly.

I looked, up surprised and nervous, straight into his cool blue eyes.

He leaned in towards me and my heart skipped a beat. He closed his eyes and I was just about to close mine when I saw something glowing in the trees behind him. I jumped up.

In the bushes was Casper, silent and judgmental. His eyes were ablaze and the frown on his face told me that everything he saw was being reported back to Blake. I turned away from him and Sebastian and went over to my backpack, mechanically looking through it, just for something to do.

A few long silent minutes later, Blake returned, his arms full of wood for a fire. Casper and Bea silently emerged from the shadows. Both were frowning at me. It was clear that everyone was aware of what had happened and I could feel their eyes on me. Tension was high and the air was silent. I felt like it was me that everyone was blaming. Thoughts were racing through my head bitterly and Bea was replying reproachfully.

'It isn't fair, it was an accident.'

'I don't know what to think Saffron.'

'I wasn't thinking; it just happened. It felt nice that Sebastian said that about me. Blake never called me beautiful.'

'Why should he? You two are just friends. It isn't his job to call you beautiful.'

'But then why is he so upset with me now, Bea? Just because he didn't trust Sebastian and I did? It's not my fault he has trust issues.'

'That isn't fair Saffy. If you had his family you wouldn't be able to trust people easily either. Besides, you know how he feels about you.'

I let Bea's last comment hang in the air without a reply. It was cold and we were all huddled around the fire, glaring at each other in turn over the flames. I couldn't tell what the boys were thinking, only that they weren't good thoughts. Neither of them were looking at me anymore, just staring at each other. I felt a moment of relief at being out of the spotlight before I realised that Bea and Casper were both still glaring at me. I glared back at Bea but she said nothing more so I moved onto Casper. I cowered slightly at his gaze. There was pure hatred in his eyes. His eyes flashed red then he blinked and looked away. I wasn't sure what to make of what I just saw. I stared at him but there was no sign of red again. Deciding it was just the reflection of the fire in his eyes, I looked away from him. The fire was dying and I began to shiver. Eventually Sebastian went to get more firewood, leaving me and Blake alone. I couldn't take the silence anymore.

"I see you are having me watched by Casper now."

My voice was conversational but the venomous look I was giving Blake told him he was in trouble.

"Any particular reason you thought it necessary to keep an eye on me?"

"Probably the same reason you had Beatrice follow me," Blake retorted. We glared at each other.

"To keep you safe not to snoop on your personal life!"

My voice was no longer conversational. It wavered with emotion as I frowned at him.

"I was trying to protect you too!" Blake cried out.

"From what?" I said incredulously. "Sebastian? He's not dangerous

Blake. What do you think he was going to do?"

"Kiss you," Blake said quietly. That stopped me short. It sucked the anger right out of me.

"What did you think he was going to do?" I asked again slowly. I wasn't sure I had heard what he had said properly.

"I was scared he was going to kiss you. I don't trust him but I saw you two had a moment over the water and I just don't like him at all."

"Blake?" My words were softer now. "I don't want to fight with you. We never fight. Please?"

I stood up and walked over to where he was sitting. I held out my hand for him to shake. He took it and pulled me onto his lap and gave me a hug.

"No more fighting," he agreed into my hair.

***

I dreamed that night too.

Saffy is back at the stream with the boys, fishing.

This time I could tell I was dreaming. The water moves too slowly and everything looks slightly distorted as if I'm already under water. I focus back on dream me.

Blake is talking to Saffy. She listens

But I don't understand him.

Saffy asks him to say it again.

I still don't understand him.

Saffy is frustrated in her lack of understanding. She shouts at Blake and
he pushes her hard.

I watched as dream Saffy jumps away from Blake, over the rocks. I watched as dream Saffy over balanced. And I watched as dream Saffy fell in the water.

Once in the water everything seems clearer. The world is no longer distorted and colours seem normal again. But Saffy can't breathe. The water is suffocating.

Above Saffy the boys both dive into the water. They are coming to save her. They both grab an arm each and begin to swim. She looks up to where Bea is waiting for her. Saffy watches her get farther away. She realises they are taking her away from the surface. Saffy tries to kick away from them, struggling to break free from their arms. The boys are dragging her down. It is useless trying to fight, they are both too strong and their grip on her is tight. She can't breathe so she stops struggling and lets them pull her down. Saffy looks to where they are taking her.

Caspar's eyes in the rock bed below grow bigger and his mouth grows wider as the boys swim, dragging Saffy into her watery grave. Casper's mouth shuts behind them and he begins to laugh.

I awoke aching and unsure if it was a dream that had woken me or the uncomfortable floor. I rolled over, trying to find a more comfortable way to sleep. I faced the fire pit and shivered. It looked like the fire had died quite some time ago. There was nothing but ash now and the air seemed slightly damp but maybe it was just the cold. I could hear the water lapping against the rocks and somewhere in the trees a night bird called to its mate. There was rustling in the trees that forced me to become more alert. I closed my eyes and watched for Bea's report. It was Sebastian.

He was awake and coming through the trees with an arm full of sticks. Behind him Blake came through the trees also carrying sticks. I saw them through Bea as she flew over head, coming towards where I was laying alone. They placed them by the fire pit and began rebuilding the fire. I heard a crack and smelt a lot of smoke then my eyelids began to glow as the fire was revived in front of me. I lay still preferring to pretend to sleep rather than talk to the others tonight. I couldn't shake the feeling my dream had given me and so I kept my eyes closed. I could hear them whispering to each other and I couldn't tell if it was an argument or just a conversation. I listened harder.

"So, you're afraid of the water?" I heard Blake say.

"And you're afraid of bugs," Sebastian retorted.

"You like Saffy."

Blake wasn't asking anymore.

"And you're in love with her aren't you?"

There was a moment of silence before Blake replied.

"Don't you dare tell her. If you do, it will be the last thing you ever do."

There was clear anger in Blake's voice but Sebastian sounded amused when he replied.

"Oh believe me she already knows you love her but that won't stop her falling for me. I won't tell her, your secret's safe with me. It doesn't benefit me to talk about you at all."

This conversation was confusing me in my half sleep state. The fire was warming me up again, making me a little bit more comfortable. I stretched and rolled over. I watched Bea watch the boys from where they sat the other side of the fire as they froze and watched me move. Without saying another word they both lay down and went to sleep. As I fell back asleep images of the dream swam past my eyes as the conversation I had just listened in on rang in my ears. Trying to ignore them both I slipped into an uneasy sleep.

Chapter Seven

Rhymes, Ruins, and Rock falls

The next morning was painted pale yellow by the warm morning sun. After we had eaten the last of the bread and fruit for breakfast, everyone was much happier. We packed up and re-entered the thicker part of the woods. There was a skip in Sebastian's step and he whistled as he walked. His happiness was contagious and soon we were all grinning and bouncing as we walked. It started to feel like old times, the times when Blake and I would go hiking and start singing a silly song to keep us going.

"Down in the jungle where nobody goes,
There's a boogie woogie washer woman washing her clothes,
With a scrub scrub here and a scrub scrub there,
The boogie woogie washer woman washing her clothes.
Tiddledy tie tie
Shaboogie Shaboogie
Tiddledy tie tie
Shaboogie Shaboogie
Tiddledy tie tie
Shaboogie Shaboogie
The boogie woogie washer woman washing her clothes.
Yes Sir!"

The time went along much faster while we were singing and teaching Sebastian the song. It was one I had learnt years ago from my grandmother when she was still alive. She had taken me to a museum and we saw how people used to wash their clothes way before even the first washing machine was invented. My grandmother told me that they used to sing songs to help them pass the time whilst doing such boring and hard work. She said they used to pass on these songs mother to daughter and soon joke versions of these songs were created by the kids to sing in the play ground. She then sung 'the boogie woogie washer woman' in the middle of the museum. Everyone clapped her little performance and it became the song we would sing together. I never forgot the words and one day while hiking I was singing it under my breath and Blake made me teach it to him too.

We repeated the nonsense song over and over as we climbed a hill. We were just singing the first 'tiddledy tie' when we reached the top of the hill. We faltered and the singing stopped short.

The hill broke free from the trees, showing a vast view of the woods all the way to the distant mountains. But none of us were looking at the mountains. We were all looking closer to us. Down the other side of the hill, a little ways away from where we were standing was a village. Without anyone speaking we all broke out into a run, Blake in the lead. We ran towards the village as fast as we had run away from our own town.

We slowed to a walk as we entered the border gates. We were immediately surrounded by ash. On every side of us were empty spaces where houses used to line the streets. A few scorched beams were still standing, creaking in the wind. As we moved closer to the village square the buildings became stone. These too were destroyed, crumbling ruins of their former glory. Great stone pillars were lying on their side, walls nothing but dust and a few bricks here and there clinging to each other without a hope of surviving the test of time. We clambered through the rubble and emerged at the centre of the village. No one spoke as we stared at what our brains couldn't comprehend.

Where the village green would have been was a large square patch of freshly turned soil, the size of a football pitch. Around the edge of the pitch were the skeletons of old buildings creating tombstones for the pit. It was impossible to know how many lives had been lost here but the village was big enough to assume it was a lot. It reminded me of that history lesson which seemed so long ago. I pictured the pile of shoes and the other pictures from the slideshow. I couldn't believe the history of a war hundreds of years ago was happening so close to home. Something I had thought was so irrelevant had come to haunt me in a living nightmare. As we tried to wrap our brains around this, Casper and Bea flew off, searching for any sign of life.

Everywhere was ghostly quiet.

I couldn't look any more. I had to turn away. Beside me Sebastian was crying quietly and Blake was staring vacantly at the ground. He wasn't looking at the grave; I gathered he was watching what Casper was seeing. Bea's own thoughts were fleeting pictures of the village from the sky as she searched for life. I focussed back on the ground. There just beyond my feet was a piece of paper. I walked to it and picked it up.

It wasn't a piece of paper, it was a family portrait. The family smiled up at me from a garden in full bloom. It gave a sense of summer, of warmth. The edges were all burnt from fire, a harsh and unbearable heat. I walked around the grave to the top and placed the photo on the ruined steps of what was once the town hall.

"I never thought this would happen so close to home," I said quietly to thesmiling family. "I'm so sorry. I had no idea. We never heard anything about this, not in the news, not at school. We should have fought for you. This disaster is bigger than any I have ever heard of on the news. History will forget you, for no one remembers individual stories when there are no survivors to tell your tale. Our education fails us when we are not told of the horrors in our own land. Why was this hushed up so?"

I turned to face the boys. Neither of them had moved away from the grave although Sebastian had sunk to his knees, still crying. Blake looked up at me, expressionless. I walked over to him and saw that he was shaking. His face portrayed no emotion but his body gave him away. I stumbled the last few steps over to him and hugged him tightly.

"This could have been our town," I said softly. My voice was muffled as my face was pressed against his chest.

"I won't let anything harm you Saffy," he whispered back. His breath was warm against my hair and he squeezed me closer to him.

"This is what happened to my town," Sebastian said from the floor.

Shakily he stood and looked over at us. We broke apart. Blake walked over to Sebastian and put a hand on his shoulder. He looked into Sebastian's watery eyes with a fierce look on his face.

"I promise you, we will find out who did this and we will get him for it."

Sebastian sniffed and shook himself.

"Come on, we should get moving."

We turned our backs on the grave and slowly moved through the ruins, retracing our steps to the gate at the border. Climbing up the hill again, no one looked back. None of us spoke or sang, we just walked on through the never ending trees.

As we moved on, the land became flatter and the trees that were once so dense became further apart. The trees themselves were growing in size. We were obviously at an older part of the woods where trees were hundreds of years old. The trunks were so large we could all hide behind one trunk and no one would know we were there. They towered above us, still and silent giants.

We stopped for a break in the shadow of a large tree.

"We are almost at the end of the woods," Sebastian said.

I looked around me. The trees certainly were getting thinner and it was less dark now that the sunlight could get through the gaps in the branches. After we had all had a rest and some water, we continued on. We were close and we could all feel the excitement and nervousness building. We seemed to be feeding off each other's emotions. Bea was practically dazzling from all the excitement. The end of the woods felt like a victory, as if getting out would automatically get my father back, as if that would be the end of our adventure. We knew this wasn't possible but the feeling was hard to smother.

It wasn't long before we came to the edge of the woods. Ahead of us was another vast meadow. The grass was long and burned yellow from the sun. There were no flowers and the ground below our feet was hard. With no sign of any wildlife, all was still. Even the birds had taken wing and flown off without even a note of parting song. We looked left and right. There was no cover for miles. We would be completely exposed. In a blur of green, Casper was gone. Sebastian and I looked at Blake quizzically.

"He's gone to scope out the land, see if there is any threats," he explained. After a pause he continued. "Casper gives the all clear. Let's go, but keep an eye out for anything."

We walked forward on the diagonal, following the direction Sebastian had pointed out. The grass was taller and burnt more yellow up close than I had first seen. Clearly it hadn't rained here for a while. We walked at a steady pace, our heads constantly on a swivel. I knew we were close to Dad. I could feel it. We were out of the woods and so the castle had to be close. It just had to be. Suddenly I started running. I wanted to get there, to find my dad. The boys started running too.

"He must be close," I called behind. "There's no danger, don't panic. I just have to get to my dad."

We were a fair distance from the woods now and something was emerging on the horizon. I ran faster, leaving the boys behind.

"Wait!" Sebastian called from somewhere behind me.

"Keep up," I panted. "We are almost there!"

"No Saffron! Stop!" he yelled back.

Suddenly I was grabbed from behind and pulled down to the ground. I lay on the ground panting hard and rolled over to look. Sebastian had pulled me down to the floor just before I fell off the edge of a cliff. I peered over the edge cautiously. The walls were smooth rock without any sign of footholds. If someone were to fall there was no way of climbing back up- If they even survived the fall. The gap was wide and without any sign of a bridge, the depth dizzying without an end. Heart hammering inside my chest I watched as several stones fell where I clung to the ground. Darkness loomed up at me and swallowed the stones up. They made no sound so I was unsure if they hit the bottom or if there even...

"Does it end?" Blake asked nervously.

"Not that I can see," I replied. My voice echoed off the stone walls.

"But then how do we get to the castle?" Blake asked hopelessly.

"Look!" Sebastian pointed. "Over there. See the stone pillars? Maybe we could use them as stepping stones."

"Are you insane?" I asked incredulously. "Those things are over a thousand feet high! Or higher! Who knows!"

I looked at the pillars trying to calculate how high they would be. It was impossible to tell; they gave no sign of ending. It appeared like they could go on forever. Logic told me there must be a bottom, it couldn't possibly go all the way down to the core of the earth. But as I looked down and watched the darkness expand and decrease, I couldn't help feeling that if I fell, I would keep falling for eternity. The thought had me shaking all over: I was never a fan of heights but falling shocked me into fear. A thin chilling mist was spreading over the darkness and between the pillars.

Heights and darkness...

"It looks like death," I said quietly.

Not only was I skittish when it came to heights but I was also never very good at long jump. A little short for my age I was fast and, thanks to all the adventures Dad, Blake, and I went on, I was strong but I was terrible at jumping. At school Blake would always laugh at me when it came to athletics. His jumps were always at least double the length of mine. This worried me as I looked at the gap between the rocks. I wondered if Blake had noticed or even thought about how bad at jumping I was. Bea whimpered in acknowledgment of the truth. We could die trying to cross to find my dad. When the thought of Dad crossed my mind, I stiffened my resolve, took a deep breath.

"All right, let's do it."

The first stepping stone was barely apart from the cliff face. We just had to step on. Nervously we stood there staring at it. It looked stable. Completely made of rock there was no chance that it wasn't solid enough to hold us but without knowing what it was standing on, it was a huge risk to step on to it. We all hesitated wondering who would step on it first. We waited. As no one moved I closed my eyes and stepped on to it alone. I held my breath but nothing happened. I turned around and looked at the boys. Seeing that nothing had happened to me, they both seemed a little more relaxed as they stepped onto the rock too. The minute we were all on the stone, we could hear whispers, and the mist intensified.

"What is that?" Blake asked.

"What are they saying?" Sebastian murmured.

Both boys seemed entranced by these whispers. I couldn't hear what they were saying any better than the boys but whatever was happening to them, wasn't happening to me. I didn't know what to do; they were both acting so strange.

"I'm not sure," Blake replied in a distracted voice.

He crouched down and stuck his head over the edge, reaching as far as he could go. He looked like he was going to fall and he didn't seem to care that at any moment he could lose balance and fall into the nothingness below. A cascade of stones crumbled from underneath him as he stretched farther and farther over the side.

"Guys! Get away from there!" I screamed in panic.

Neither of them seemed to hear me.

Sebastian was leaning down now too. I pulled at their clothes but they brushed me off.

'It's not working!' Bea said to me in panic. 'Maybe you should...'
Her voice trailed off but I saw the picture in her head and acted on impulse. I smacked them both over the head. It wasn't hard but it was enough to snap them out of their trance. They sat on the ground in a daze while I grabbed a pair of headphones from my schoolbag. I shoved them quickly into Sebastian's ears and went to Blake's backpack. He also had a pair and I did the same for him. They looked at me with more life in their eyes and smiled gratefully. I pointed to the next pillar.

It was further away than the first one and we had to put a bit of effort onto the step. Immediately after leaving the stone, the whispering stopped and I pulled the boys headphones out of their ears.

"What was that?" Sebastian said shakily.

"I have no idea but let's not go back," Blake replied.

"Let's move on, quickly," I suggested.

We stood up and made to leap to the next stone but as we did, the stone started to sway and a rumbling sound was coming from the dark below.

"What's going on?" I cried over the sound.

"It sounds like an earthquake!" Sebastian shouted back.

I looked at the boys' horrified faces just as a huge crash sounded behind us. The stone pillar we were just on was crumbing down into the dark below. The noise was reverberating within me as I watched Blake mouth the word 'GO'. We all stumbled to the edge of the stepping stone and leapt for the next one just as the one we were on began to shake violently.

The noise did not stop when we got to the next one like it had before. The earth was still shaking and the rumbling was still coming from the dark below. We got to our feet quickly and took a run and a jump at the next one. This was the last before we reached the other side. We got up and ran to the edge. We could see the cliff face on the other side. This was the farthest gap we would have to jump. We threw ourselves into the jump, knowing it was life or death. The boys made it fine but I felt myself falling before I had gone far enough over the gap. I screamed as I fell past the top of the cliff. I scrambled and grabbed hold of the edge. The stone was rough against my hands and it was still shaking strongly. I could feel my hands slipping from the rock. I willed them to hold on longer but it was just no use. My hands slipped and I began to fall. Just as I let go of the rock, a hand grabbed hold of mine. I was slammed against the rock face and roughly hoisted up over the edge. My face felt like it had been scratched with sandpaper and I could feel my knee was bleeding through my jeans but I was alive and on solid ground.

I turned to the boys who were panting heavily. Blake looked at me with frightened eyes but Sebastian came over and looked at my grazed cheek.

“Are you alright?” He asked.

“Well I’m alive.” I said shakily.

‘We almost died, of course I’m not alright!’ Beatrice said in our head, almost defiantly.

‘Hush.’ I thought back, ‘He just saved us.’

‘How do you know it was him not Blake?’ Bea retorted.

‘Look at Blake’s face and tell me he saved us.’ I thought sadly. Bea looked at Blake. I looked too. He was looking down at the ground with a sad and slightly angry look on his face. He was having a conversation with Casper.

‘Looks like they are fighting.’ Bea said in a soft voice. I turned away from Blake and smiled at Sebastian. Taking his hand I said quietly

“Thanks.” He smiled at me and squeezed my hand.

“Anytime, Saffy. I’ll catch you every time you fall.”

We looked to where we were going. In the distance we could see a dark, ominous lake with a huge fortress of a castle, looming over it. I let go of Sebastian's hand, moved over to Blake and helped him up. The three of us stood there staring at the darkness we were about to encounter.

Chapter Eight

Heads up

The grass was shorter this side of the valley so we could see all the way to the castle. It loomed in the distance on a small hill, blocking out some of the sun. There was no cover; soon whoever was in the castle would be able to see us walking towards them. We started walking slowly on. With every step I took I could sense my father getting nearer. I couldn't bare the suspense.

It felt like forever had passed by the time we reached the castle. Together we stood on the edge of the moat, looking into it. The dark murky water looked cold and forbidding. It was nothing like the river we had to cross before. This water was still, stale. It gave no atmosphere of calm as the river had done. It made me shiver although the sun was still out. Standing in the mud I looked down to the water's edge. A thick layer of green slime floated on the surface. There was no way to see my reflection in this water. I couldn't see who I was through the scum. I couldn't check I was still me. I didn't want to get into this water. The water was clear of sludge further into the middle but it was still impossible to see if anything was in it.

"No drawbridge," Blake said looking up at the empty archway of the castle. "I guess that means if we can cross this water, we can go in."

"But how can we cross the water? I'm not swimming." Sebastian answered slightly panicky. Blake looked at him in a most unimpressed way.

"You won't have to. If you had looked around properly, you would have seen the boat." And indeed there was a boat just fifty metres away from us, bobbing close to the bank. We ran over to it. It was a small rowing boat, smaller than a car, with two oars. The paint was chipped and it was clearly old but it was floating and didn't seem to have any leaks.

"Looks pretty stable, I don't see any holes and it seems to float fine." I said to the boys.

"Do you think it will hold us?" Blake looked it over.

"I think we should try it, all together. After all," he looked sideways at Sebastian menacingly

"I'm not afraid to get wet."

I glared at Blake but said nothing. He jumped in and sat down with an oar. I got in and grabbed the other. Nervously, Sebastian clambered in and sat at the front, looking at the castle. The water was like glass, icy black with no indication of how deep it was. It was still, barely a ripple was seen as a slight breeze ran over its surface. The wind sent a shiver down my back as I looked for some kind of trap or obstacle that we had to pass to get to the gate. But there was none that I could see. Surely it wasn't as easy as just rowing across. I looked down into the water and saw only a distorted reflection of my own face in the dark below. We began to row. Even this was perfectly synchronised as Blake and I had often gone out in his father's old boat together during the summer. That was years ago. After his dad died the boat was wrecked and his mother wouldn't let him in another.

Despite the years passed we were still just as in tune with each other. If it had been under a different circumstance, I would have almost enjoyed being back in the boat with Blake again. But the fear for my father stopped me even from smiling. I looked down into the water and that is when I dropped my oar.

As I looked down I saw, not my own reflection looking back at me, but someone else's face. I gasped and looked in horror at the boys. They were looking over their sides of the boat into the water too. I looked further out into the water. We were surrounded by floating heads. Stunned I turn back to my side of the boat. All those heads- so many heads- floating in the water. I looked down into the wide, blank, staring eyes and imagined the horrors they had seen to have ended up here. The shadow of their last screams were still whispering through their open mouths, showing jagged teeth and rotting gums. The air had gotten colder as I stared into a pair of dead, staring eyes of a little girl. Feeling sick I dragged my eyes away from hers and turned back to the boys in the boat.

"So this is what happened to all the missing people." I said quietly.

Suddenly I realised that this was bigger than trying to find my dad. Looking at all these dead people I knew, we couldn't just find my dad. We had to stop the rebels from doing this. I couldn't believe how many people had already died. It didn't make sense that the rebels were killing off so many people when we were told they were trying to build an army. The news said these people were being taken by the rebels but why would they take s many people from their homes just to murder them? Was it to send a message? But it couldn't be that, no one had found the rebel's hideout except us. It just didn't make sense that the rebels were the ones behind all this. I began doubting all the stories I had heard on the news as I saw for myself the damage that had been created so far by unknowns. It was easy to watch the news and believe the stories when it was happening so far away yet now that it stood before me, I couldn't believe this was all down to the rebels. The rebels wanted to take down the government so why should they kill people who could have been part of their army? But still I was relying on information from the news. What if the rebels didn't even exist? What was The Authority trying to hide? Staring across the water at all of these heads, all these dead people, all of these forgotten lives, I wondered who could possibly justify so much destruction.

Sebastian was frozen, unable to take his eyes off of the dead people. As I watched a tear fell from his eye into the water. The tear drop caused a ripple, constantly expanding through the black glassy water. We needed to keep moving forward. I nudged Blake to get him to start rowing again. He jumped in fright and I watched in horror as the boat rocked scarily from side to side. Sebastian screamed as he became face to face with the head he was staring at. I yanked at his clothing and pulled him back further into the boat. He sat curled up on the floor by our feet, whimpering.

"Let's move on." I said to Blake. His eyes were glazed over as he nodded once and began to row.

When we reached the bank, Blake and I grabbed Sebastian and hauled him out of the boat. He collapsed at our feet, shaking. I sat down with him and put my head between my legs, willing myself not to faint. With my eyes closed I could see all of their faces again silently screaming at me. I opened my eyes and stared at the dirt, keeping my head down so as not to pass out. From about five metres to my left I heard Blake throwing up on the side of the bank. None of us had seen anything like this before and none of us were taking it well.

I closed my eyes and pushed out the images of the heads so I could link to Bea. I could see myself with my head between my legs, still as a statue and breathing slowly, next to Sebastian who was still shaking. Blake was on all fours a little ways away, heaving into a bush. Bea looked around for Casper but couldn't see him. I felt her worry but I pushed it away. I couldn't think about anything right now, I just had to focus on breathing and not fainting.

I could feel the blood circulating properly in my head again and very slowly sat up. Blake was walking over to where Sebastian and I sat. Sebastian didn't acknowledge us at all. He didn't move, just sat there, shaking. I stood up to talk to Blake.

"Where's Casper?"

Now that I no longer felt faint I could appreciate Beatrice's concern for his whereabouts.

"He's up there somewhere." Blake gestured into the sky. "I wanted someone to be on lookout while we were all so vulnerable."

I looked at him in surprise. Even when incapacitated, Blake was still thinking of protecting us. I had never valued just how much he took care of me but when I looked around and saw how we had left ourselves open for an attack, I saw how practical he had been by putting Casper on guard.

"Even when you're throwing up you're still looking after me." I said smiling at him but wrinkling my nose at the words.

"We should be thinking like soldiers if we are really up against an army here. I don't like being out in the open like this." We looked at each other then at Sebastian where he still sat next to me. Evidently he had completely ignored our entire conversation.

Fear does strange things to people. Our fight or flight instincts should have evolved to a more superior function. We should be able to deal with fear better than we do. The minute we freeze when sensing danger is the minute we gamble with our lives. Sebastian was gambling now with all of our lives. We needed to get him to move. I pulled on his arm but he wouldn't budge.

"Come on Sebastian, we have to move." I said in an urgent voice. He was crouched on the floor, arms wrapped around his knees, rocking slightly. He was muttering to himself in a constant stream of whispers. He was barely stopping for a breath, I couldn't understand it but the word 'no' came floating up to where Blake and I were standing so often I wondered if he was actually saying anything else. I looked at Blake helplessly.

"We have to get him to move." He said.

"He doesn't look capable of that yet. I don't know what to do." I replied.

"We're not safe here; we're totally out in the open."

Blake was looking around nervously.

"I don't know what to do," I repeated. Blake looked down to where Sebastian was crouched and grabbed his arm. He pulled on it but Sebastian didn't move.

"Stop it, you'll hurt him!" I said to Blake.

"You try and get him up then!" Blake said angrily. "We have to get out of here, we are way too exposed." I bent down and stroked his hair. Cupping his chin I forced him to look me in the eyes. Sadness stared back at me.

"Please." I whispered. Shakily he got up and we moved into the shadow of the castle and in through the archway.

Through the archway we walked. It opened up into a courtyard, brightly lit and filled with plants. A light breeze cooled my skin yet it was not unpleasant. The plants rippled and there was birdsong all around us, yet we could see no birds. Looking around me I could see nothing but green in every direction. We followed a pathway that ended up at a wishing well. It was all so beautiful and peaceful I could feel myself relaxing every second. The horrors behind us seemed like a distant dream.

Inside my head Bea began to giggle.

I looked into the wishing well. The bird song had sounded like it was coming from inside it but now that I was beside the well I could tell that it was coming from somewhere else. I looked around trying to find the source of the song.

It was no longer bird song; there seemed to be words to the music now although I couldn't make out what they were saying. I looked to the boys; they were looking around confused too. Bea was no longer laughing, sensing something more sinister behind the song. Blake began walking into the plants, off the path. None of us spoke, none of us wanted to break the spell. Sebastian and I followed Blake. The light was shooting rainbows amongst the plants. It didn't make sense until we stopped short and I saw the cause of the rainbows. We looked ahead. And we looked back.

Ahead of us was a wall of mirrors. The song seemed to come from behind the glass. Blake stepped forward and stared into his own reflection. He said nothing, didn't move, and just stared. With an expressionless face he slammed a rock into the mirror, shattering it into a million glittery pieces. Just as the rock was about to make contact with the glass I could have sworn I saw the reflection of Blake smile.

The smashed glass tinkled to the ground and the singing stopped. Blake turned to us, slightly pale but triumphant to have stopped the confusing sound. The slight smile on his face faltered as the mirrors all around the smashed one glowed and reflected a picture of him. All along the wall was Blake, over and over again, all singing the haunting song with no words.

Blake broke into a run along the wall, smashing every mirror in sight but still his reflection sang on from more and more of them. The slight breeze we could feel before was still just as light to the touch yet had forced the plants to bend and buckle as if they were in a hurricane. With every mirror Blake broke, the light became darker and darker. With a shock I realised it had begun to rain. The plants and the ground that had been glistening with glass were now wet with rain and as I looked up I could see the rain falling from the sky. Yet we were dry.

As Blake realised what was happening he ran back to us, as dry as Sebastian and I. Thunder rolled above us and a few moments later, we were lit up by a flash of lightening. The plants around us were almost horizontal in the wind that still felt like no more than a breeze to us.

"What is going on?" I had to raise my voice in order to be heard over the untouchable storm.

"I don't know." Sebastian replied looking up at the sky with a worried expression on his face.

"We need to get out of here." Blake said, leaning in towards me so I could hear what he was saying over the wind.

"This isn't natural; we must have triggered some sort of alarm. Whoever it is knows we are here now."

"It was probably you smashing all those mirrors that did it." Sebastian said.

"Not very subtle really."

Despite the storm everything seemed to go quiet as Blake looked at Sebastian with pure, passionate rage. Sensing a fight brewing between the boys, I spoke quickly, hoping to distract them before things got worse.

"It doesn't matter now. Right now we've got to move."

We ran back through the plants to the path.

The beautiful old wishing well was snow overflowing with water, green and stagnant all over the path. We splashed through it, following the path hoping it would lead us to where we needed to be. This paradise had so quickly changed to a nightmare and it woke me up, reminding me why I was here.

Dad.

We ran on, still haunted by the singing, now accompanied by the wind and thunder. Another flash of lightening illuminated a door and we ran towards it.

We burst through it and slammed the door shut on the storm behind us. We were all still dry except for the sweat and tears dripping down our faces from the fright run. As we caught our breath we looked around at what fresh nightmare we had entered into.

Chapter Nine

Things that go bump in the night

Our footsteps echoed to the pulsing beat of dripping water and the wind whistled through the cracks in the stone. It sounded like a very creepy orchestra and it gave me goosebumps. Everything was cast in shadow although the source of the light was undetermined. The stone walls were slimy from the water and everything was cold. It was quiet after the storm in the courtyard. There were no signs of it this side of the door. I looked up but the ceiling was the same as the walls- grey damp stone. It was impossible to tell where the walls ended and the ceiling began, it just seemed to curl up like a great, stone tunnel. Everything was quiet. As we walked through the tunnel we could see a door up ahead. Nervously we attempted to open it, assuming it would be locked. It wasn't. I looked to the other two; they were staring wide eyed into the gloom. The dark is simultaneously terrifying and soothing. To walk in the unknown allowed us to forget about everything. Out of sight, out of mind. It was easier to feel unafraid when there was nothing there to be afraid of. However, before long, my mind began playing tricks on me. The dark became a home to every monster my mind could make up. Peering into the dark I could have sworn I saw the dark peering back.

"Well." I said shakily,

"I suppose this is the only way in so we might as well go."

Nobody moved.

"It's just a little dark that's all, we aren't afraid of the dark eh Saffy? Haha..." Blake tried to sound like he wasn't scared but his voice cracked and wavered. His laugh echoed into the darkness and ended in no more than a whisper. He stepped forward, Casper following him, on full alert. I grabbed Sebastian's hand and followed him in.

As soon as we had stepped through the doorway, a gust of wind slammed the door shut with an almighty bang. We were left in the dark. The room was so dark there was nothing to see. Even Sebastian's blond hair right in front of me was swallowed by the shadows. It was cold too and the air was wet. It made the room feel so big, like it went on forever. I squeezed Sebastian's hand in fear and whimpered into his shoulder. Brazenly, Blake strode on. We could hear his heavy footsteps moving away from us. His footsteps weren't echoing like they would in a big room. It was very disorientating to not even manage to gauge the size of the room through the dark. It was impossible to tell exactly what we were walking into.

"Come on Saffy." Sebastian said softly in my ear. "It'll be ok, think of your dad and how much he needs you right now."

His words threw a picture of my dad into my head and I forced myself to start moving.

It was not quiet in this room. Were we even in a room? It was too dark to tell. What must have been the walls were rustling all around us. In front of us we could see the faint glow of Casper and Bea. Neither of them were giving off much light; both were pale as they registered the cautious feelings Blake and I were experiencing.

"I can't see a way out." Blake softly called back to us. He had reached the wall opposite the door we had entered through. There was no door. But the wall seemed to be moving. With the faint light of the personalities, I looked closer and screamed.

The wall was covered in insects. But not regular insects, oh no. These were huge: thick beasts that glared at us, clicking pincers and flicking tongues. Their long legs were tangling in a maze of limbs and yet each one moved about on the wall, over and under each other, fluidly. My skin crawled as I stared in horror at what I knew was my best friend's worst night mare. Spiders the size of my head were crawling over earwigs that must have been nearly a metre long. At my scream the rustling stopped. There was a silence as all the insects looked at us and we stared back in horror. Then all at once they began to move.

"Run!" Sebastian yelled as a spider got ready to make the leap onto Blake's back. We all sprinted away. From behind us were swarms of beetles, ants, spiders, millipedes, earwigs, woodlouse, all at least ten times bigger than their natural size. The fear was too much and I cried as I blindly ran for my life. Sebastian pulled me along faster than I could run and I tripped, falling forwards. I felt my hand slip out of Sebastian's and I put it out in front of me to break my fall. I scrambled to my feet and began running again. The fall had hurt my ankle and I stumbled along as quickly as I could but the insects were gaining on me quickly now.

The boys were ahead of me and I cried out to them in a panic. The scuttling of hundreds of legs was deafening. At my cry the boys both looked over their shoulders. Despite his fear of bugs Blake turned and sprinted towards me, closer to the beasts in pursuit. Sebastian stopped and watched in horror as Blake ran towards his fear to help me. He grabbed my arm and put it round his shoulder, put his arm around my waist, and began running again. I was all but lifted off of the ground by the speed of his run. Tears were still running down my face from fear but I wasn't in pain. Sebastian started to run too as we began to catch up with him.

Casper glowed brighter than I have ever seen him glow before despite Blake's fear. His light allowed us to see the door. Just as we burst through it something clamped down on Blake's leg. White with fear, he collapsed dropping me to the floor. I grabbed his arms and pulled as Sebastian ran at the big hairy spider. Its legs were wrapped around Blake's knee, pincer's clicking. Sebastian tackled the spider and I listened to the crunch of foot meeting flesh. Blake's face was white as a sheet, his eyes wide with fear and his mouth open in a silent scream. I gripped tighter onto his arms and stared into his eyes. I felt the spider's grip on Blake falter and yanked him out of the doorway. There was a thud as the spider fell to the floor. The door slammed shut. We lay on the floor panting, Sebastian standing over us.

"Are you ok?" Sebastian asked Blake, looking over at the door instead of at him.

"Yeah,' said Blake. He was also looking at the door, the ghost of fear still clear across his face.

“What was that?!” I said in a shakily indignant voice. “What kind of person lives in a castle with those...those beasts?”

“A mad man.” Sebastian muttered quietly. He looked at the door again and then looked around the room, eyes landing on the dead spider on the floor. I looked at it too. It was almost as big as me. Jet black with all eight hairy legs stuck out in odd directions. As I watched, it twitched, making us all jump.

As I looked closer I saw something wasn’t quite right about its body. I walked over to it and rolled it over with my foot. Blake groaned at the sight of its underbelly. By turning it over I had revealed its head which had fallen under the belly when Sebastian had killed it. All of its eyes were still wide open in a haunting stare.

Ignoring Blake’s groans I looked into the eyes of this beast. Something was odd about one of its eyes. I moved closer to it and realised what it was. I kicked the spider back over, hiding its face, and jumped back.

“It’s a camera!” I said to the boys.

“What?” Said Blake from the floor.

“There was a camera in its eye! Someone is watching us. Someone put a camera inside that thing’s head so it could watch us get chased by these things!”

“That really is sick. That thing almost killed me.”

“Actually I don’t think it could have.” Sebastian said, bending over the spider’s corpse. “I don’t think it’s actually real. Look.”

I looked at where he was pointing and saw that the hair had come away from the body, showing metal where there should have been flesh. It didn't make any sense to me.

"Why would someone make fake giant insects to guard their castle?" I asked.

"Technically it is an arachnid." Sebastian said, gesturing at the spider. "And how do we know they are all fake?"

"What do you mean?" I asked, looking at him in horror.

"I mean this might have been the only one with a camera in it. The others might really be giant bugs."

The thought that we were being watched for all of this time freaked me out. Somehow that seemed scarier than all the mutantly huge bugs in the next room. The question of who it was doing all of this was still at the forefront of my mind but now I knew that they knew who we were I was nervous. If they knew who we were and why we had come they could do something really bad to my dad.

"Who do you think has been watching us?" I asked the boys quietly, not even looking at them.

"It doesn't really matter. All that matters is that we have to go in again, there's no other door."Sebastian said. I looked at him incredulously but it was Blake that spoke up.

"Are you mad? I'm not going back in there." Sebastian looked at him and then turned to me and held out a hand.

"Think of your Dad, Saffy."

"This is so much bigger than that, Saffy!" Blake looked at me. "This is'nt just about finding your dad anymore. This is the place where hundreds maybe thousands of people have been kept and killed. You saw all those heads out there! How many towns have been wiped out by this monster? We can't do this alone anymore. We have to go back, report this to The Authority. These rebels can't get away with this!"

The look on Blake's face was more than terror now, it was anguish. It wasn't just creepy crawlies that were getting to him, no: I could see he was scared for our lives and what would happen to us. He could see this was real, that there was a high chance we really might die here looking for Dad. But something he said made me stop. When he mentioned going back and reporting this to The Authority I realised he still believed everything he had seen on the news. He had seen all the things I had seen and come to a different conclusion.

Perhaps he was right and the rebels were behind all of this. If that was true then reporting to The Authority certainly would be a good idea. But I couldn't help feeling that he was wrong. He was scared and I knew why. I was scared too but I didn't think going for help would be a good idea. If I had thought that would help, I would have gone to The Authority when Dad first went missing instead of going to Blake, or again when Sebastian told us he knew where everyone was being held captive. There were so many times we could have turned around and gone for help but we never even considered it before now. It was all too much. I didn't know what to do. How was I to save my father? Suddenly I felt very insignificant and I doubted my ability to go on. I looked at Blake, then up at Sebastian who was still holding out his hand to me. Then I looked at the door. I knew door. I knew that behind there was Blake's worst nightmare.

‘Bea,’ I whispered in our head. ‘Help me, I don’t know what to do.’

‘We’ve come this far.’

‘But I can’t ask Blake to go back in there. What if something happens to him?’

‘You can’t do this without him Saffron. You need him. But I don’t think he can go on any further. Look how pale Casper is right now.’

I looked over at Casper. He was barely even visible, completely drained after fighting to stay bright when we needed him. His glow had gone as he hovered near Blake, still panting on the floor.

‘So you think I should turn back?’

‘I think going forward will be the hardest thing you will ever have to do. Is it worth it?’

I thought of all we had been through to get this far. We never thought it would be this hard to find my dad. I guess we didn’t really think at all when we left. It seemed like a whole lifetime ago that we were in the meadow complaining about school. We had been through so much since then. We had been shot at, got lost in the woods. I had almost fallen to my death. We had met Sebastian and seen just what might happen to our own town. Blake and I had been through so much to get here. I was here for my dad but I had pushed Blake so far and I didn’t know why he was still going along with all of it. We had been through so much, seen such terrible things but I couldn’t stop now.

“I have to find my Dad,” I whispered out loud, finally answering Bea and replying to Blake in one. “We’ve been through so much to get here and

I can't do this without you Blake."

I looked him in the eyes. Through the dirt on his face I could see that he was still pale from fear but I watched as his dark eyes hardened and he nodded.

I took Sebastian's hand and he pulled me up. Once I was on my feet he then extended his hand to Blake who ignored it and got to his feet himself. Sebastian looked at Blake like he was impressed with him but Blake didn't see. He was too busy brushing himself down. I realised he was having a conversation with Casper and wondered what he had to say. Casper didn't look happy. It was clear he didn't want to go back through that door. I supposed he didn't think it was worth it. I glanced at Sebastian. He was still looking at Blake in a funny way. It was admiration. That I could understand: it was impressive that Blake would go in there again. Insects had been his private fear since before I could remember. He agreed it was irrational for the most as they were pretty harmless but coming up against such beasts as those who were attacking us, ready to kill, justified his fear. Some other emotion was laced in with Sebastian's expression. It seemed like desire but also sadness. I wondered what Sebastian was thinking about to look at Blake that way. The look was calculating and I didn't really understand it but before I could dwell on it, Sebastian spoke.

"Last time the insects didn't bother us until you screamed Saffy," he said in a rather business like tone, turning away from the door and looking from Blake to me. I blushed sheepishly.

"It's not your fault, you were surprised but it also means we'll know this time that we have to keep very quiet." We all nodded at Sebastian's words so he turned to open the door.

"Wait," I said. Sebastian's hand hovered just above the door handle. The boys both turned to look at me, questioning my outburst. I wasn't really sure why I had said something. I knew that sooner or later I would have to go back into that room but something made me stop. I knew what it was; anything that could stop me from going back into that room would work. I really didn't need much of an excuse.

"What is it?" Sebastian asked me.

"I... I don't know," I faltered. Blake looked at me sympathetically but said nothing.

"I guess I just needed a little more time. It's hard to go in knowing what is there."

"I know what you mean," Sebastian said putting his hand on my arm. "It was easier to go in when we didn't know what we were going to face. But now that we do, it doesn't really change anything. We still have to go through that door whether we like it or not. There is no other way through."

We braced ourselves by the door, knowing what was on the other side. Quietly Sebastian opened the door and we followed him inside, hardly allowing ourselves to breathe.

Chapter Ten

The caged man

There was nothing there. The room was empty. We breathed a sigh of relief as Casper and Bea both glided around the walls and illuminated a bug free room. I could feel the relief from Blake as he relaxed; Casper grew brighter with every second the truth was dawning on Blake. I knew how he felt but I wasn't relaxed yet. With all the fear we had faced I knew this wasn't the end.

On the left wall, close to the corner near the wall that we had entered in was the door that would get us out of the room. No wonder we hadn't found it when we ran through here last time, it was nowhere near where we looked. We walked towards it quickly, paused, and then quietly opened the door. This room was well lit so we could see that we were standing in a huge room with animal cages in rows and rows.

"Does anyone else find it odd that none of these doors are locked?" Blake asked, looking back at the door rather than at the cages. No one answered him. We were too busy staring at all the cages.

And the cages were staring back.

In every cage there was a human being and their personality. I walked over to the closest cage. Along the row I could see all the personalities were water spirits. The man in the cage stared up at me with wide eyes from the cage.

He was starved and grey but did not look hurt; just haunted.

"Who are you?" he whispered. The fear in his voice was clear, this was a broken man.

"My name is Saffron," I said quietly. "I've come to help you."

"Help me? What more can you do for me? I'm too far gone. I have been here for four years now. Don't waste your time on me, help them." And with that he pointed feebly at the rest of the room. I slowly turned around in a circle.

In the water spirits row there must have been a hundred cages and as I looked closer, I saw that they were all men. The next row was all air spirits and again, all were men. There were a hundred of those cages too. I walked along the length of the room. Each row had about a hundred cages: men with earth spirits, women with water spirits, women with air spirits, and women with earth spirits, all lined up row after row.

"Where are the fires?" I heard Blake ask behind me.

"We never see anyone with a fire spirit here," a woman's shaky voice answered.

"He must use them for something."

"He?" Blake asked the woman.

"Yes," the woman answered. "He is the one doing all of this."

"The leader of the rebels? Who is he? The Authority don't know who is leading the rebels, maybe if we found out we could pass on the information. We could stop this war."

"Saffy," Sebastian interrupted,. "Your father, what's his spirit personality? Maybe he's here."

My stomach twisted. I had completely forgotten about my dad with the sight of so many people. Blake was right: it was bigger than I thought. But with Sebastian's words I started to look for my dad again. My father had an Earth personality and so I started going down that aisle. Man after starved man, I peered into all their faces, hoping to recognise just one. I was at the end and getting desperate when I stopped and sunk to my knees.

"Dad," I whispered. My eyes immediately started to water at the sight of my usually so polished and full of life Father, grey and sunken on the floor. He looked like a ghost and his personality, once so bright and green, now looked almost transparent and grey. He looked up from where he half lay on the floor.

"It is humorous," he said weakly. "They starve me and then torture me with hallucinations of my own daughter. What more can they possibly take from me? I see her there now, staring at me in horror and fear at what I have become, but there nevertheless. Oh my Saffron, how I wish I could see you once more!"

Tears streamed down my face as I reached through the bars. I could sense the other two standing behind me but I couldn't care about that now. They merged into the background, as unimportant as the bricks in the wall. All I could see was my dad.

"It is me, Dad. I'm really here."

His eyes unfocused and refocused as he looked at me. I saw a hint of life flow back into his face as he stared into my tear filled eyes.

"Oh! My darling girl! What are you doing here? It is not safe."

He reached out for the hand I had stretched out to him and we both sobbed uncontrollably as our hands found each other.

"I had to find you," I managed to get out between sobs. "Blake helped me get here to save you."

At my words Blake stepped forward and put his hand through the bar to hold Dad's other hand. We sat there, three humans and three personalities, crying with joy and sadness, just completely overwhelmed.

I was so happy to see my dad again that I didn't notice that Sebastian had gone. I realised with a jolt that sitting and crying wouldn't help my dad now that we had found him. I stood up and looked at the cage door. It was locked with a simple key hole. This gave me hope. I smiled and looked at Blake. He looked shocked to see me smiling in such a situation but shock soon turned to puzzlement as I pulled at his backpack.

"Look at the lock Blake, you can pick this. It's as simple as the one back at the office!"

The puzzled look on his face turned to determination as he pulled his back pack off his back and unzipped it. He turned his back pack upside down and emptied the contents out onto the floor. He fumbled through all the stuff in his bag until he found his set of tools. They seemed like a bundle of flat, skinny knives but each one had an odd looking shape on the end.

Blake examined the lock for a moment then picked out two of the funny looking tools. The first one was a flat thin knife looking thing that was bent at a right angle. He chose this and another tool with a bit of a hook at the end. He put the tool with the right angled bend into the keyhole first then began working at the lock with the other tool. It was all a bit fiddly for me to comprehend so I turned my attention back onto my father.

Holding his hand I told him about our adventures: of the woods and the ruined village, the beasts and fishing. Everything seemed to melt away as I talked to my father of the horrors we had faced. I grew tired just telling him of our adventures.

My stories of our adventures were accented by the sounds of Blake working on the lock. It was taking him a long time. Out of the corner of my eye I saw him change tools again. I looked down at him; he was frowning over his tools as he tried to figure out which one to use.

"What's wrong? Why won't the door open?" I asked him.

"I don't know," Blake replied frustration clear in his voice. "It just won't. No matter what tool I use, nothing works!"

I looked at my father in desperation. Tears welled in my eyes as he quietly smiled.

"You must leave Saffron, you too Blake. It is not safe here. I am sound in mind as long as I know you two are safe but if you are captured there would be no more they could do to hurt me. You must leave, you must stay safe."

I shook my head vehemently as he spoke.

"I'm not leaving you here! We went through so much to get to you. leaving you behind now that we have found you!"

My father smiled yet his voice wavered slightly as he replied, "Yes dear, you did find me and I am so proud and grateful but I cannot let you stay here and be captured yourself. leave and find someone who can help us all." He looked around at all the cages. "There is nothing you can do for us here Saffron and you are no good to anyone if you are captured." He looked at Blake. "Please, take my daughter away from this place."

Blake nodded at my father and put his hands on my waist, trying to pull me away. I clung to the bars of my father's cage sobbing. I couldn't leave him behind now that we had fought so hard to get here. I couldn't believe that Blake could so easily walk away.

"Come on Saffy." Blake said into my ear. He lifted me off my feet and carried me, screaming, away from my father. I lost him amongst the cages through my tears. Blake carried me to the other side of the room and through a door into a corridor. This wasn't the way we had come in. I stopped crying and looked at Blake in surprise.

"I couldn't get the lock open. So let's find something that will."

His eyes sparked with determination. It wasn't over yet. I hurriedly wiped my face free of tears and looked around. Blake and I were standing in a blank corridor with Casper. I called out to Bea in our head, asking for her location. She showed me pictures of cages.

"Beatrice has stayed with Dad, he doesn't know she is there but we want to stay close to him."

Blake nodded.

"Stay in touch with her, don't let her get too far away from you, we don't know where we are going or what we will face, you don't need that extra stress of the distance."

I nodded in agreement and lead the way down the corridor. It was as we walked that I suddenly realised.

"Where is Sebastian?" I asked Blake.

"I'm not sure. Last I saw he was looking up and down the cages. I thought he must be searching for people from his own village."

"Oh... Maybe he found someone then, he must be still in there."

"We'll find him when we go back in. He can help us free everyone."

Blake shrugged off Sebastian's absence. I focussed back on the task at hand. We slowly walked towards the first door in the corridor. Blake sent Casper through the wall.

"It is empty, we can go in," Blake said quietly. I breathed a sigh of relief and opened the door. We walked into a store cupboard.

"This is no good," I said to Blake.

"We are never going to find anything in here to help us. Those bars were too thick to break through, we need a key."

"Well we are never going to find a key in here," Blake said sighing. He turned towards the door.

"We might as well head out."

Casper flitted out through the wall again and a moment later Blake said, "All clear, let's go."

We headed back out into the corridor and walked along to the next door. It was spooky that the place seemed so empty; for such a big castle, there didn't seem to be anyone actually working here. It all appeared very modern too; it was all out of place for the building it was in. The next door was exactly the same as the other; there was no indication that this room would be more than a store cupboard like the last. Blake sent Caspar in before us and a moment later opened the door into a completely empty room. We walked in and closed the door anyway, just in case we were visited by someone who worked here. Not that there seemed to be anyone working here at all.

"This is no good, there is absolutely nothing here!" I exclaimed in quiet desperation. It seemed like we would never find anything that would get my dad out of his cage. I could feel myself beginning to cry again and I willed it to stop. Crying wouldn't help anyone right now.

I called out to Bea in our head. 'How is he doing?'

'Same as before, frail and sad, but holding on.'

'Are you ok? I'm not too far away am I?'

'No, you're ok for now but be careful. It will hurt a lot for the both of us if you stray too far away.'

'I know. I'll stay in touch.'

As a kid you are told that straying from your personality will hurt; that you can only withstand a short physical distance between you until it causes serious pain. Naturally once you are told this information you become curious as to how far you and your personality can handle before it hurts. Everyone has tried it at least once. I remember being impressed by how far away I had got from Bea until searing pain entered my head and heart. This is how they had managed to catch the personalities along with all of the people in the cages. Although they could not touch the personalities, they would never willingly put themselves and their humans through so much pain by leaving their side. Bea and I were testing our limits with every step I took away from her.

It was pointless to stay in this empty room so once more Casper was sent to check the corridor. It was clear and so Blake and I moved on. This corridor was distressing: the uniform of it all was making me a little crazy. All the doors were exactly the same with no indication of what was behind them. The walls were white and blank of any windows or pictures. There were no ornaments or furniture. It was impossible to tell if you were even walking forward unless you focussed on an upcoming door.

We walked straight into the third room without even checking. We hadn't seen anyone since we had arrived and I doubted there was even anyone in the castle other than those trapped in cages and ourselves. We had walked into a security office of some sort which would usually have made me laugh given that it was unlocked. But this was no time to laugh. There were monitors on the walls showing different corridors, all exactly the same as the one outside this door. There was also a desk.

We ran over to it checking for a key. Excitedly I pointed to one pinned up on the wall above the desk. It was an old fashioned ring of about twenty keys. We grabbed it and left running back down the corridor. We were so excited at finding the keys that neither of us saw the steaming mug of coffee on the desk or considered the fact that if the corridors were monitored, we would have come up on one of those screens.

W sprinted back down the corridor and through the door that put us back in the room with all the cages. Bea breathed a sigh of relief in my head as the tension eased between us. Keys in Blake's hand we ran back down the row of cages to where my dad was sitting in his.

Chapter Eleven

The Rebellion of the New Age

My father looked at us in awe which soon turned to fear.

“I thought I told you to leave! How many times must I tell you that it is not safe? How am I to keep you safe when I am trapped in here? Your poor mother must be worried sick,” he said in desperation.

With a jolt I realised I hadn’t thought of my mother at all. With all my focus put on running towards my dad I had never thought about how I was running away from my mum. But I couldn’t think about that now. Not now I was so close to releasing my dad and the both of us going back home to Mum. I realised that I had also ripped Blake away from his mum. It flooded me with guilt and pain. I thought of Sebastian’s story and how his mum was dragged out onto the street and shot. That could have already happened at home and I had just run away from it all; left Mum unprotected in a town full of Authority Guards. I had run to my dad to save his life but what if I had run away from Mum when she needed me most? And Blake’s mum too. Both left unprotected the minute we ran away. We hadn’t thought out our adventure at all, neither of us had planned on being away for so long. Never in our most wild dreams would we been able to prepare for what had happened to us or what we had done and seen. I pushed all that aside and replied to my father.

"You didn't really think we were going to leave you here? After we had come all this way! No, we found a key, look!" I excitedly explained to Dad. I reached back through the bars and helped him to his feet while Blake went over to the lock. There were so many keys to choose from on the ring, it would take him a while to figure out the right one to unlock the cage but once he had found it, I was confident it was the same key for all the cages and we could free everyone.

While Blake was working on the lock once more Dad told us what had happened to him. Throughout the time he was talking he never once looked at me, as if he couldn't quite bring himself to talk about such things if he knew his daughter was listening. After all we had seen on our travels to get to Dad I doubted he could say anything to me that would shock me anymore than what I had already seen. I supposed that when Dad saw me he thought of home, of Mum and safety. He saw his daughter, his innocent little girl, even if I felt like a warrior, in his eyes, I was still just a princess. His story took him to a different place. I wondered what he was seeing in his mind as he spoke. His personality's colour was flickering from a strong green to a ghost of sliver so faint he almost disappeared completely. As he spoke I realised why.

"I had been researching these disappearances for over a year before they started occurring in our town," he began shakily. "I had just left my office when they took me; big people and many of them. I could not tell you who they were even if I wanted to because they put a bag over my head. I tried to fright but in the dark of the bag I was disorientated and then they hit me hard over the head. I did not wake up until I was here, in the cage. I talked with the others in the cages all around me and all their stories were the same. No one knew who the operator of all of these events was. All they knew was that no fire personalities ever came through here and every week a man in a hood would come through and take six people: a man and woman from each spirit section. Those chosen were never seen again."

"It's true," the man in the next cage spoke up, shakily. "My village was also attacked by these people although we did not know whom they worked for."

He got to his feet and moved over to the side of the cage that connected to my father's. He was dirty and very thin. His face was taut and grey. He looked up at me with haunting eyes, the ghost of his traumas etched into his soul.

"They came for us in the night. We had no warning; no news of this had reached us before this. We were a simple village in the woods with no connection to the outside world. They came and they took and then destroyed everything. I remember I was sitting in my house with my wife when I heard screams from further out of the village. It was dark but there was a faint orange glow coming from the border. The fire spread quickly. The village was dry so the wooden houses caught within minutes. Everyone fled to the other side of the river but we didn't all make it. They were waiting for the few of us that did. They came out of the trees in masks, some on horseback, some on foot. They surrounded us easily, there weren't that many of us who had escaped the flames. Some of the villagers tried to run and some tried to fight. They were shot point blank. The rest of us quietened down after that. They tied us up and drugged us and we awoke in these cages. One by one I've watched the rest of the village leave and not come back. Those who weren't chosen have simply died in their cage: too hungry to fight; too exhausted to ask for food." As he said this he faltered, lay on the floor, and closed his eyes.

I gasped in shock as I realised he was talking about the village we had found in the woods. Images of the burnt village lying in ruins and of that giant grave scorched into my mind and were brought up in my memory. I could feel Blake's arm shaking next to me and wondered if he was seeing the same thing I was.

"It was the same for me too," a man in a cage behind us said. His air personality was so faint we could barely see him.

"It was the same for all of us."

The man in the cage next to him stood up and spoke.

"They always came at unexpected times and always in a hood or mask. None of us know who took us or what they took us for. We have all been trapped in these cages. Nobody knows anything."

"How can we when they knock us out every chance they get?" a voice further along said.

We had a bigger audience than we realised. Everyone was listening into our conversation. Hope was spreading around the room by Blake and his ring of keys. I searched around for who had spoken. It was a woman in the row behind the earth's. She seemed stronger than the others. Her water personality seemed to be bluer than the others like she hadn't been caged as long.

“But why are they doing this Dad?” I asked him.

“My research brought up some interesting theories on that matter.” Dad said. He sounded stronger once he started talking about his research and there was a light in his eyes that wasn’t there before. “I suggest it has something to do with the rebels of the new age and their fight with the traditionalists.“Years ago when that fight first began it was to prevent the control The Government had over the people. The rebels believed that fighting The Government would fix the problems with the way the world viewed social class. Back then it was not just men over women but the personalities had a hierarchy too. Fire were the strongest and the only ones in charge, water was next in line then earth and finally air. The rebels tried to fight but The Government beat them back every time. The rebels eventually managed to fight for equality between all personalities after much bloodshed. But the new government, The Authority as they are now called, was not a lot better than the first and many of the traditions continued to stand. None of the original rebels survived this new government. Now the children of the new age, these new rebels, fight these old customs without knowing just what kind of world they are fighting in or for. This rebellion, I believe is the reason we are being taken. I think that they are trying to build an army.”

I stared at my father, stunned. I couldn’t comprehend what he was saying. An army? It was silly speak. Of course, our area had an army training base; all areas had to have one, but it was unlikely we were ever expected to actually use it. Things like that didn’t happen in areas like ours. No one would ever need an army where we were from. Armies were for the places that came up on the news; people fighting over food or land or oppressors. Civil wars were all that were ever heard of now. Our histories once spoke of wars where the whole world would get involved but soon the people realised that millions dying for one man's greed was ludicrous and so each country agreed to leave each other alone. Civil wars within countries continued but no one ever died for an international wrong doing again. There hadn't been an army in our area for years. The Authority rendered armies useless as they had their guards. As I thought of this my mind brought up pictures of the ruined village we had found in the woods. Of course, if they had had an army perhaps they would have lived and whoever had attacked them would have been brought to justice. I knew now that the media didn't always tell us the whole story and sometimes, like with this village, they didn't tell us any of the story at all. Yes, I used to think that things like that didn't happen in areas like ours but now I knew differently. Blake spoke up, pausing in his work at the lock.

"Who is creating the army, the rebels of the new age?"

My dad just looked at him.

"It's not the rebels doing this," the woman spoke up through the row of cages between us. "I was the leader of the rebellion. We found out what was going on in the area and came to see how we could help. The rebels are trying to help the missing people, we would never do this to so many lives. In order to try and help we had to find out where everyone was being held captive. As the leader I volunteered to go underground, to get caught and so lead my people to the prisoners. I haven't been here long. The rebels are thinking up a strategy as we speak to overthrow this evil minded monster!

We just have to get enough followers to help us win this battle. We need as much man power as they have in order to stand a chance."

Blake looked quizzical.

"So the news was right when The Authority told us you were building an army?"

"Yes. It is perhaps the one thing that they have got right about the rebels."

"But then why would you build an army against The Authority?"

The woman laughed at Blake's question.

"You are kidding right? Look around you. This is why we need an army. Tell me boy, do you feel safe at home? Even before all of these people were abducted and you were living a normal, ordinary life, can you honestly tell me you were happy? You look like you are close to finishing school so had you figured out who you were going to marry? Were you happy with the customs you were forced to live by? This is why we need an army!"

I thought about how we had been planning on running away from all of the Authority's rules. It was impossible to deny that she was right. We had wanted to rebel against The Authority too, in our own way.

"So it really is The Authority that have done this to all of these people?" Blake asked in disbelief. His face showed how much he couldn't comprehend the concept of a government that didn't do what was best for their people."

"The Authority Guards. They are all fire personalities, every single one of them. I've never seen a Guard that didn't have a fire spirit. It's the strongest of the old government."

Blake looked at me in horror.

"So the Government is doing this? They are the ones taking people from their homes and starving them, killing them?"

"I believe it is worse than that," my dad answered quietly. "I think they are trying to manipulate our personalities."

"Manipulate?" Blake asked in a voice that expressed a lack of understanding and fearfulness. Getting the cage unlocked had now been completely forgotten as this new information was thrown at us.

"Manipulate is the term used in many of the old books on personalities, that describes the act of changing ones personality for instance from earth, to fire. As fire is the strongest of the personalities it is beneficial for someone with a weaker personality to manipulate theirs into a fire. Once someone had an army of fire personalities, the old regime would come back and fire would take control once more.

"However, from what I have read, manipulation is a tricky process. It is almost impossible to create a formula that will work and naturally. There has never been anyone in our history that has managed to do it. It is a theory most dangerous and painful. The concept of changing the ghost of what one's soul decided one was from birth is difficult. The process would have to start by stripping one's own personality of its form before branding it with fire with such force it forgot it was ever anything else other than that. It would force one to forget everything about who you were previously. As you will have guessed that process comes with great harm to oneself so if they really are attempting to manipulate personalities here, we have great reason to fear. It is said that, should the theory become a reality, most would not survive the pain of transformation."

We looked at him in horror. And then I spoke, quoting the book from Dad's office: "'For we are nothing without our personalities and without us, they are also nothing.' They are creating an army of fire personalities? That's why all the guards have fire personalities: they have been changed, manipulated, so that they could join! That means that The Authority is the one doing this to everyone?"

"Not exactly."

Sebastian spoke behind us. It made me jump. Other than the first time I had asked Blake where Sebastian had gone I had completely forgotten about him. With all the excitement of trying to get Dad out of the cage and free everyone else, Sebastian had slipped my mind. I spun around to look at Sebastian. He had managed to creep up on all of us with none of us noticing him. As Dad was at the end of a row of cages, no one behind bars could have warned us that he was coming. He approached us with a Guard on either side of him. For a fleeting moment I thought he had been caught and sold us out and then I realised that there was no fear in his eyes. Instead, Sebastian was smiling straight at me. That was the last thing I saw before I was thrown into darkness as my head was covered.

I closed my eyes and watched though Bea's eyes as Blake's head was covered too. He fought against the darkness so both Guards had to hold him down. I struggled, trying to get the thing off my head so I could go and help Blake. I heard my dad cry out behind me but Bea showed me that he was ok, no one had touched him. He was just helpless, still locked in his cage, the keys lying forgotten on the floor.

The next thing I felt was a needle in my arm and the rush as something was injected into me. I fell into a hallucinating half sleep, mixing memories and dreams alike.

I was learning to ride a bike for the first time with my dad. The bike was going faster and faster as I peddled hard. I was riding along when my Dad disappeared.

> *Frantically Saffy searched for him as the grass turned into water. As Saffy peddled she sank deeper and deeper. The water was cold yet not particularly wet against her skin. Saffy was fully immersed and yet could still breathe.*
>
> *Saffy landed on the bottom, got off her bike, and began to climb the wall in front of her. She didn't question why there was a wall underwater. Nor did she question that it took an awfully short time to sink yet was taking a very long time to climb. Saffy was not afraid of falling but she was frustrated at the slowness of her limbs.*

As I broke the surface, I kept climbing and suddenly realised Blake was next to me climbing the same wall. I was faster now than I was while I was under water. I looked around. The water had gone from beneath me and I was in town climbing my father's office block. When we reached the top we began running, jumping buildings

and cliff tops alike

until we were no longer running on concrete

but back in the long grass again.

The constant change of scenery was jarring but it never affected my step as I ran. The long grass whipped around my knees, stinging my bare legs. For a brief moment I wondered why I wasn't wearing jeans like I usually was. But I was more interested in running than what I was wearing.

No matter how fast Saffy ran, she just wasn't getting anywhere. She pushed herself to run faster and faster but the grass slowed her down. Water appeared on her left. It was different to the water she had been in before. It looked foreboding and choppy – angry at the sight of her running. She swerved to avoid it but then fire burst into appearance on her right. Hot and fierce, the flames licked at her ankles. She swerved again to avoid that. She ran on the thin path left between the cold depths and the fiery hell. In front of her was another cliff edge. Beyond it was black; there was nowhere to even attempt to jump to. There was only the fall. Something told her it was not safe to turn around. Saffy was trapped and the only escape was the darkness beyond she just had to choose which way to get there.

Chapter Twelve

A Traitor amongst Us

When I came to, I was in yet another room of the castle, tied to a pole. I looked around me for Blake and my dad. Dad was in yet another cage at the opposite end of the room to me, Blake was tied to a different pole next to me. Bea and Casper stood at our sides unable to help, unwilling to speak. The room was huge, bigger by far than the town hall. The smallest sound would have bounced off of the walls had the room been empty but it wasn't. All around the room were computers and cabinets. Each monitor was flashing different coloured buttons and the fans were whirring, creating a hum of white noise. On some of the computer screens data was showing. I saw a list of towns on one with numbers next to it; another had what seemed to be different formulas on it and the one after that had all sorts of information and numbers on it. I didn't understand what I was looking at.

The door opened and in marched six Authority Guards in their red uniforms. Their personalities marched with them. They spread out along the wall, three either side of the door. There would be no chance getting past them even if we could get untied. The Guards said nothing to us and looked ahead of them, expressions blank. Their eyes were unseeing and they didn't look at us anyway. I didn't recognise any of their faces but I didn't really expect to. It wasn't often anyone from our town became an Authority

Guard.

A woman opened the door. She was tall and slender in a full length dark green dress. As she walked her footsteps explained her height; she was wearing very high heels. With every second step I caught a flash of leg as a slit in the dress opened all the way to the knee. I looked up into her face. Her mouth was open in a smile, her red lips highlighting the bright white of her teeth. She was looking at Blake with her dark brown eyes. They were heavily defined by her makeup, making her eyes look darker. I watched as her staccato footsteps carried her across the room to stand in front of Blake.

She reached out a hand and held his chin forcing him to look at her. Still smiling she said nothing and neither did he. I noticed her long fingernails were painted the exact same shade as her lips. She laughed and walked off to a television on a wall. She turned it onto the news and watched for a while. It was the headlines discussing all the missing people and The Authority reassuring people that they were safe regardless of the facts. The same blame game with the rebels at fault. The woman turned her back on the television and spoke to us. Her voice was crisp, cold, and commanding.

"Don't you love the news? So much free advertising! They incite fear and panic before I have even stepped out of the house. I've profited from their panic before I've even had my first cup of coffee, I do enjoy other people's terror, don't you? It is so nice to be paid to do something you enjoy. I enjoy exploiting people's fears."

Her eyes flashed and she grinned before adding, "I'm good at it too."

Fear was building inside my chest as Sebastian walked into the room.

He grinned at me and moved over to a computer. He started typing on a key board, looking at a screen and talking quietly to the woman. Bea was flitting around now, agitated and unable to keep still as I tried to piece together what was going on.

"I don't understand!" I called at Sebastian. "You're working for the bad guy? Why?"

The woman laughed again as Sebastian stopped what he was doing on the computer and slowly walked towards me. I wrestled against my ties but they wouldn't budge. Whatever was binding me was tough and digging into my skin. I fought against the pain and kept struggling. I could feel something wet on my hands and tried to figure out if I was bleeding or just sweating. Sebastian was in my face now. He was angry and his eyes flashed as he fought for his own purpose.

"I'm not working for this bad guy everyone keeps talking about! There is no bad guy. There is only me and what I hope to achieve. You see, nothing I have told you was true. You never noticed the obvious thing did you? I would see it in your eyes, and in yours Blake."

Here he turned and walked towards Blake. He stood as close as he could to Blake and spoke straight into his face.

"You never noticed what was right under your nose. It is unbelievable that you never noticed what was different about me. Both of you willingly let me stay with you, slept by me, lapped up every little bit of my pathetic sob story, and trusted me through everything. I saved your lives and led you right to the castle. I can't believe you followed me blindly. Apparently it is a true, love really is blind. You were too busy in love with Saffy and so you never noticed, I have no personality."

His voice was calm yet smug. A smile played across Sebastian's face as he watched our faces react to the truth.

I gasped and Blake groaned. It was so obvious now that something had been said. It was undeniably stupid that neither one of us had ever figured it out when Bea and Casper where constantly there, highlighting what wasn't there to highlight.

"This was never about you or me or The Authority. This was about my brother. You see," Sebastian continued, walking away to grab a chair and coming back to sit a little ways away from us. "Every now and then in this world a cruel force of nature occurs when a baby is born deformed. In the case of my brother a simple slip of a chromosome count meant he had no personality. My uncle, a scholar aware of the passage you so eloquently quoted before Saffy, convinced my mother that she could not keep such a crime of nature. He convinced her that the baby could not survive and so must be put out of its misery. And she let him."

With these words Sebastian stood up and threw his chair across the room. The metal clanged on the floor. It tumbled over and over; the sound reverberated around the room. This sudden act of violence made me jump. I flinched away from Sebastian and the chair. Sebastian clenched his fists, breathing heavily and stared at the chair. Angrily, he turned back to where we were tied up.

"My pathetically weak willed mother allowed my uncle to kill her son, my brother just because his personality was not visible to them. But I saw it, it was clear to me that my brother's personality had been born inside of him; I could see it in his eyes. And they killed him anyway.

"Since then I have been determined to prove them wrong, that we can survive without our personalities. My uncle was wrong and now he pays for it. I have him here, working for me. He has no choice, I am the boss." Sebastian grinned manically.

I looked at him in horror.

"So you are stripping people of their personalities?"

His smile faded.

"Well no. Honestly I have only been successful once and that was on me. But I have a theory as to why that worked. You see, I think my invention needs a blood link between the subject and the operator. It worked on me because my uncle was the operator. So far I have not managed to use the right combination of the same direct bloodline but it seems my luck has changed."

He looked from me to my dad in the cage across the room.

"So that's why you helped us find your castle! You needed Saffy," Blake growled from his pole.

Sebastian didn't answer. He just laughed. The woman joined in. She looked up from the computer and spoke, "It wasn't just your little friend we were interested in, it was you. You see, Sebastian had this marvellous idea and yet had no way of working it out himself. He needed a financial backer; that's where I come into the story. I've always been incredibly wealthy but I wanted something more. I was rich for the sake of Riches but now I get to be evil for Evil's sake. And that," she looked directly at Blake, "Is so much more fun."

"But what about The Authority?" I asked Sebastian desperately.

"Oh well that really was a little piece of genius on my behalf. You see, I approached them and told them my plan. I told them I was attempting to make a breakthrough on the strength of the bond between human and personality. I told them that not only was I going to prove that people who are born with a specific genetic order- resulting in the personality being internally based- were totally normal and just as deserving of the title 'human being' as the rest of us, but that I could also build a personality manipulator and give them as many fire personalities as they wished for their little war. Marie has helped me pay for all my study. Money is where the power is in this world and she knew that having The Authority on our side would just make sense for a good business. Marie has always had good business sense, that's why she's so rich."

"And now," she added delightedly, "I get to go to all of The Authority's swanky parties too."

"You see, they are as eager to control the people as I am eager to prove my uncle is a murderer!" Sebastian continued.

"But you are murdering hundreds in the process!" I yelled at him.

His face fell a little. The sadness in his face was so openly vulnerable that it made my heart falter. His eyes were full, life times of sadness and horror cried from within. I realised why as he spoke quietly.

"Five million six hundred and forty three failures so far but I know, I just know that I have figured out what is wrong this time. It's all about the blood! So Saffron, if you'd be so kind as to operate on your father to prove this theory, everything will be right again."

"She's not going to help you! Nothing will ever be right for you again! You're sick! You're a monster!" Blake was yelling, furiously fighting against his bonds. Casper was flittering around, unable to stay still, the darkest green I had ever seen him.

Sebastian turned to the woman.

"You see Marie; he is definitely the one you want."

"You are right Sebastian, The Authority will be very happy with him." Looking at Blake she continued, "We have been watching you Blake; your story is sad but you are strong anyway. We have manipulated your surroundings to test you. I have paid millions to see you suffer, to see how you would respond. Your father's death, your hatred of bugs, your love for this girl here, all of it has been a test. How far would you go for what you thought was right, how far would you push yourself? We thought we had lost you in the castle with our giant bugs- did you like those by the way? I paid for them and thought they were rather juicy- but as much as you hated it, you pulled through. You have stamina that is very deeply wanted. Your strength to get past all fears is what we need. You have been chosen to help The Authority. You will be rich beyond your wildest dreams. And everyone knows that where there are riches, there is power. You should join voluntarily."

Her eyes flashed as what she didn't say loomed between us all: if he didn't accept he would die.

With defiance in his eyes, Blake spat on the floor but stayed silent. Marie sighed and walked away back to the computer. Sebastian looked at

Blake with that same look I had seen on his face after we had escaped from the bugs. This time I understood the look.

"You're a strong guy Blake. But tell me, how is it that someone with an earth personality is afraid of bugs? Or better yet, tell me how anyone with an earth personality has the ability to have such fierce feelings? It is my opinion that your earth personality does not suit the spirit it has been given. I think it is time we changed that."

Sebastian moved over to one of the cabinets and opened it. Inside were vials, all with a lava looking substance inside. He took one out and attached it to a needle. My heart was pounding in my chest as I watched Sebastian walk over to where Blake was struggling. Sebastian pushed the needle right into Blake's heart and injected the lava in.

I screamed and bucked against my bonds, trying with all my might to get over to where Blake was slumped against the pole. Casper stopped flitting around. Ever so slowly he began to turn a darker green until he became brown and from that to a red clay colour. Then all at once Casper burst into flame and Blake screamed.

Tears were streaming down my horror struck face as I watched Blake go silent and stand to attention, his eyes red and unseeing. Sebastian untied Blake and yet Blake did nothing.

"You see?" Sebastian said, "I have found a way to manipulate personalities. I can make them whatever spirit I want, I just have to change the formula. And now that you have seen that work, it's your turn to work for me."

I was too weak to fight anymore.

"Blake," I whispered. He was gone. There was no sign of him in the face I knew so well. Sebastian said something to Blake and he walked over to me. As he loosened my bonds I looked over at my dad. After being starved for so long, he was so weak he could barely stay conscious through all that happened. The situation was hopeless; with Blake gone and Sebastian the bad guy I didn't know what to do. He was the one we were fighting all along. We just didn't know it. I couldn't do what he wanted with me. I couldn't do that to my own father. But if I didn't, Sebastian would surely have Blake kill us both. I could see no other way.

"Dad," I called over to him. His head lifted feebly. "I'm so sorry." Tears were constantly rolling down my face and I didn't even try to stop them.

"It is ok sweetheart, it is ok."

Dad's voice tried to be a soothing tone although tears choked him.

I turned to what was once my best friend and looked into the eyes I knew better than my own.

"I love you Blake."

His blank face stared back at me. I ran towards the needle that Sebastian had thrown on the floor, stabbed it into my own heart, and pushed. I coughed and fell to the floor. I heard a distant scream. Was it Dad, or Sebastian, or Blake, I don't know. And now I never would. The room around me blurred and then everything went black.

Chapter Thirteen

A Twist in the Tale

I awoke in my bed. I turned off my alarm and got in the shower. While shampooing my hair I thought about my dream. It was not one I could tell Blake about. I stayed under the hot water longer than normal, relaxing all of my muscles. My neck was stiff from lying down for so long.

Eventually I got out of the shower, dried, moisturised, dried my hair, brushed my teeth, and put on my school uniform. With a last look in the mirror I added some lip gloss to my lips and then walked downstairs. In the kitchen Mum was making Dad's breakfast while he read the paper, drinking his coffee while he did so. Mum turned around and Dad looked up from his paper as I entered the room.

"You look beautiful Saffron," my mother said with tears in her eyes.

Dad stood up and put an arm around Mum's waist. Looking at me he asked, "Are you ready?"

"Yes," I said.

My normal morning routine meant I was only slightly late. I couldn't help but stop and look at my parents holding each other and smiling at me.

"Let's go then," Dad said, walking over to the back door and opening it.

I looked through it and gasped. The garden was in full sunlight with rows of chairs in it. Down the middle was an aisle with a white carpet. Blossom fell lazily from the trees and butterflies fluttered around the people. All my friends and family were there, smiling at me. I looked down and saw that my uniform had disappeared.

In its place Saffy saw a white wedding gown. Her father took her arm and with the music walked her down the aisle. Standing at the front, waiting for her was Blake. Saffy was so happy he was the one waiting for her.

The ceremony was a blur. I was just waiting for the part where I could say 'I do'.

Saffy closed her eyes and kissed her husband.

***

I can't believe what I saw. She ran over to the discarded syringe and pushed it into her own heart before I could stop her. She gasped and slumped to the floor. Her water personality, Beatrice flickered and seemed to fall a little. She floated over to where Saffy was dying and slowly disappeared, her hand on Saffy's cheek the whole time.

I raced over to where she lay. She was slumped on the floor. Her eyes closed. I felt for a pulse. It was there but only just; it was getting weaker by the second. I didn't know what I could do. Tears trickled down my face as I held her and watched the last of her life drain from her body.

With a flash, Beatrice reappeared, the brightest blue I had ever seen her. She danced around the room for a moment and I could have sworn I could hear her laughing. Then, as quickly as she had appeared, she vanished from sight. The room was silent as Blake stood there staring into nothing, completely unfazed by what had just happened. The man was just lying in his cage, stunned. And I tried everything I could to get her back. But she had stopped her own heart, injected air directly into the chamber. The weakest of the elements was her murderer. I didn't want to kill her. I just wanted to show the world that my brother didn't need to die. I needed to show the world that there was no need to be afraid of people who were different. And now she is dead.

She is dead and I destroyed her best friend.

And me?

I have turned out to be the bad guy.

But it is more complicated than that because I cannot stop being the bad guy. I still have something to prove and I still have to help The Authority. If I don't, they will kill me. Is it wrong to value my life over all of theirs? It is too late now anyway. I have no personality and so I will keep finding a way to prove it is possible. I will do it for love. I am not afraid.

I will avenge my brother's death.

All those experiments still to be done... It can't stop now. I won't stop now. But I will let the man go. I will let him take her body back home. I

I will organise that now.

***

After a few days I am strong enough again. After Saffron had died, Sebastian took me out of the cage and kept me in a room. He brought me medicines and food until I was healthy enough to go home. They let me go with my baby. There was no need for them to keep her and so I was permitted to take her home. My wife would need to see her and we could give her a proper burial. There was nothing I could do for Blake and so I had to leave him behind. He was as good as my son and it broke my heart to have to leave him behind but when Sebastian manipulated him, Blake was wiped of his memories. He no longer remembered me or anything from his past life. He would not remember my little girl and for that I am almost grateful to Sebastian. Blake will never feel the pain I feel of losing Saffron. Sebastian ordered a car to take me back to my town. I am in a sleek black town car with a driver and a Guard. We are in a convoy. In the other cars are more Guards and my baby's body.

'It is time to go home baby. You are safe now.'

I walk into the living room where my wife is sleeping in her chair. She looks like she has not eaten in days. I am grateful she is safe. I have been missing for a week and I was worried that she would also go missing or become a victim of the Guards. Despite how fragile she looks, my heart swells to see her alive and in our home. I walk over to her and stroke her cheek.

"My darling. I have come home."

Her eyes flutter open. She is confused for just a second before she collapses into my arms. We do not talk for a long time. I cherish this moment as we hold each other. No words are needed as we support each other in an embrace. Finally she speaks.

"Saffy ran away."

That was the first time she had ever used our daughter's nickname. I look at her with tears in my eyes. I know I have to tell her and yet it breaks my heart to try and get the words out. One day I will tell her the whole story of how brave our daughter was as she fought to save our family but for now I settle on comforting my wife through the inconsolable truth.

"No, love, she didn't run away. She ran to save me."

"Then why is not she with you now? Where is she?"

The Authority Guards, including Blake in his new uniform, choose this time to come into the living room. Four of them were carrying a Saffy sized box. My wife cries out in unspeakable pain and collapses into my arms. I stroke her hair.

"She is home now."

"But she did not make it!! My baby! My baby is dead!" wailed my wife.

The Authority Guards put down my daughter's coffin and turned to face us, cradling their guns. They did not advance but their presence was menacing. I held my wife as she fell to pieces over our little girl. I stood there, quietly watching Blake's face. He was impassive as he stared blankly ahead, ignoring the body of his best friend in a box on the floor. At a signal I missed, all the Guards lifted their guns.

"Oh." I said. I may have made it out of the castle, but not by far.

***

I can't stop thinking about her. It was a shame she died for her father when I know The Authority will have killed him anyway. We have to protect our secret. I don't like doing this anymore. I don't want to give The Authority any more mindless soldiers for their army. I have succeeded in creating internal personalities and now I must show people that they can let these people live. I set out to prove that my brother died for nothing and now I can. Now I am not the only person living with their personality on the inside. My test subject survived and I am a success. But I am also in over my head. Marie is ecstatic with our progress. She is invited to many Authority parties and she loves all of the attention. I will never convince her to stop doing all of this.

I did this for the love of my brother but no one seems to care that I have created a formula that puts personalities inside the body. If I did that then there would be no more manipulation and The Authority wouldn't get the rest of their army. If I could put everyone's spirit inside their bodies, no one would ever know who was strong and who was weak.

There would be no more prejudices over what personalities looked like. After all, my personality was air and I have created and destroyed so much, people would assume I was fire. I need to stop The Authority's dictatorship over our land but I can't do it alone. I need Blake back.

It was shocking to see him so unaffected by Saffy's death. Especially after all I had seen them go through together. Every little mind trick that I thought up and every obstacle The Authority came up with to protect the castle, they fought through together. And now they will never be together again. I did that to him. I knew how much he loved her and I pushed in, played her, and then got her killed. I know he would have been in pieces; perhaps he would have been quick enough to stop her. I don't know. I wish I had been quick enough to stop her. She took me by surprise acting so quickly. I was in shock. I didn't know how to save her and I was too late to stop her. Beatrice's last laugh will haunt me forever.

I know what I have to do and it starts with Blake. The army shall have no more soldiers. In my lab I change the formula. It comes out a perfect earthy colour. Once Blake is summoned I inject him straight into the heart.

Eyes closed and fingers crossed in hope, I wait for the change. I open my eyes and my heart sinks. In front of me is Blake with his fire personality. I know I have failed. But then Blake spoke and my heart began to beat fast. This one word gave me the hope I needed. This one word told me I had succeeded. This one word told me we could defeat The Authority. This one word told me Blake was back.

"Saffy?"

Made in the USA
Monee, IL
04 November 2026

67386533R00075